Testimonies

"*Your Best Life in Jesus' Easy Yoke* came to me when I felt stressed out. *Jesus was relaxed, why was I anxious?* I couldn't put it down! From the opening 'Apprentice Prayer' I was hooked! I needed to come to Christ and learn from Him — Bill pointed the way. The clear teaching with engaging Scripture meditations showed me that it was possible to actually walk in the peace and power of the Lord — not by trying harder, but by training in His easy yoke and light burden."

Steve Harper
Executive Pastor of Grace Church in Cleveland, OH

"Eventually our well runs dry. Perhaps we dug into the arid ground of perfectionism, anxiety, overwork, or self-promotion. Here's a map to show us where to dig deeply into the well-spring of God's sustaining grace. I am so grateful for Bill Gaultiere, who lived *Easy Yoke* before he wrote it. He's helped countless harried leaders — like me! — drink from the life-giving waters of Jesus."

Larry Winger
CEO Provision Ministries in Irvine, CA

"Bill has taught me how to rest in Jesus' grace-filled, easy yoke. I've been sharing these insights and practices with my therapy clients and with the pastors and leaders I help in Cloud and Townsend's Ultimate Leadership intensives. We're participating in the emotional healing that God brings!"

Eileen Callahan
Psychotherapist in Newport Beach, CA

"*Your Best Life in Jesus' Easy Yoke* helped me to realign my life into the unhurried rhythms of grace. Bill does a fantastic job of helping people understand how to live relaxed, yet empowered lives in the Father's world."

Bobby Schuller
Pastor and President of the Hour of Power in Garden Grove, CA

"This book is so rich and practical. I identified with the personal stories from Bill and Kristi and clients they've helped. Being Jesus' apprentice is helping me not to be stressed out in ministry and to overcome my anxiety and hurt from the past."

Karin Mazzeo
Children's Pastor in Riverside, CA

"I'm a business guy and I love this book! Learning to abide in the presence of Christ has made me more effective in my leadership on the job and in ministry."

Lance Wood,
Tax Partner of PwC in Irvine, CA

"We used *Your Best Life in Jesus' Easy Yoke* to introduce apprenticeship to Jesus at our church. The content is rich with a vision of new life in the kingdom of the heavens! It gives a spiritual formation pattern for overcoming false narratives and daily stressors to step into the heavenly reality. The spiritual experiments and prayers have helped us integrate abiding in Christ into daily life."

Leroy and Mildred Gerner
Care Pastors at King of Kings Church in Omaha, NE

"I love The Apprentice Prayer! It's helped me release my anxiety over the day to God's loving control and given me courage. I've shared it with many people."

Ron Thompson
Lead Pastor of Twin Cities Church in Grass Valley, CA

"What a treasure *Easy Yoke* is! I'm experiencing steady healing from anxiety, fear, control and worry as I apply the lessons in this very practical book. I'm thankful and amazed at how I'm learning to relax in God's care and protection."

Kevin Koberg,
Business Leader in San Diego, CA

"I used to think the Christian life was hard work till Bill showed me that Jesus' easy yoke for me is joyful and peaceful. Now I'm teaching this to all of our Bible study leaders and they're sharing it in their groups."

Sue Wood
Teacher for Community Bible Study in Seattle, WA

"After absorbing and applying its principles in my own life for a year, I took my pastoral staff and elders through *Easy Yoke*. It's a practical, enriching, and transforming curriculum for Christlikeness. The new edition is even more engaging — I'm sharing it with my whole church!"

Steve Phillips,
Lead Pastor of The Journey Church in Irvine, CA

"*Your Best Life in Jesus' Easy Yoke* has been a field manual for me to learn how to live in the Kingdom of God as a disciple of Jesus and as a pastor to others. Bill's theological, spiritual, and psychological insights have helped me to win the battle with unhealthy emotional patterns. I've discovered how to delight in Christ even in stressful circumstances!"

Aaron Damiani
Rector of Immanuel Anglican Church in Chicago, IL

SOULSHEPHERDING

Soul Shepherding, Inc.
4000 Barranca Parkway, Suite 250
Irvine, CA 92604
Email: Bill@SoulShepherding.org

Your Best Life in Jesus' Easy Yoke is an updated edition of *You Can Live in Jesus' Easy Yoke* (2010).

All royalties for this book go to support the care of pastors and missionaries through Soul Shepherding, Inc., a 501c3 nonprofit corporation in the State of California.

Soul Shepherding offers a two-year Institute in Spiritual Formation and Soul Care with an option to earn a certificate in the ministry of Spiritual Direction. There are four 5-day retreats on Spiritual Formation, Spiritual & Psychological Development, Soul Care Ministry, and Relationally Healthy Leadership.

Visit SoulShepherding.org for free resources, books, and programs to help you thrive with Jesus in your life and leadership.

Blog: SoulShepherding.org/blog
Podcast: SoulShepherding.org/podcast

Facebook, Instagram, Pinterest, and YouTube: Follow Soul Shepherding

Your Best Life
in Jesus' Easy Yoke

Rhythms of Grace

to De-Stress and Live Empowered

Updated Edition

by Bill Gaultiere, Ph.D

Author of
Journey of the Soul:
A Practical Guide to Emotional & Spiritual Growth

With gratitude to God for Dallas Willard
who took many hours from his busy schedule
to listen to me, pray for me, and teach me
how to do all that I do in Jesus' easy yoke.

Contents

Special Features

Bible Studies, Tests, Diagrams, and *Breath Prayers*

Introduction

There's an old saying, "When a student is ready the teacher appears." I am first and foremost Jesus' student.

One of the great blessings of my life was meeting Dallas Willard in 2003. I was at the beginning of a great spiritual renewal inspired by the ministry of Ray Ortlund, Sr. to me and so I was a ready student. Dallas quickly became my "key mentor," the one God has used to unlock treasure stores of "the knowledge of the glory of God in face of Christ" (2 Corinthians 4:6).[1] His influence is all over this book.

I had spent over 2,000 hours listening to Dallas' spiritual formation seminars and had met privately with him many times when I shared with him *Your Best Life in Jesus' Easy Yoke* (the first version). He said to me: "This is groundbreaking! Pastors and others will come under this teaching and develop aspects of it in their own ministry."[2] He went onto explain his appreciation for how my book had unpacked the psychology of apprenticeship to Jesus.

Easy Yoke had a very long gestation period. Back in 1995 Kristi was pregnant with Briana, our third and last child, and the Lord led me to put a halt to writing books and going out on the Christian speaker circuit. I had published three books by the time I was thirty years old and sold 30,000 copies when God asked me to follow in the steps of Abraham and take my dream of being a best-selling Christian author and lay it on the altar — out of love for him, my family, and neighbors.

In the years that followed I went from depression ("Why doesn't God want my gift?), to burnout ("I'm tired of helping hurting people all the time."), to jealousy and anger ("It's not fair that my colleague gets to write that book!"), to peace ("Hmm. I'm not so anxious anymore."), to exuding joy ("This simple life of quietly loving God and the people in front of me is wonderful!"), to learning to bless my competitors ("Thank you Lord that *he* wrote that book — use it to bring honor to Jesus and to help many people.")

Fourteen years after going to the altar, I was hiking in the High Sierras with my son David, a teenager at the time, when I awoke early one morning before we ascended Mount Whitney. As I watched the sunrise glow on the majestic mountain I sensed the Lord speak to my heart and release me to publish books again. I felt very close to God and honored that he trusted me.

But I wasn't asking God to let me write a book. In fact, I had little ambition for it. I had learned the joy of sharing my writings freely with people who asked for them. Instead of seeking to be popular and writing for masses of people "out there" as I'd done before, I was simply sharing what God was teaching me with the pastors and other servants of the Lord that I knew.

In 2010 I published the first edition of *Easy Yoke* as a series of lessons that I offered to two groups of pastors that I was leading in Christian spiritual formation and soul care. I cared for them and trained them to use the curriculum to lead "Easy Yoke Groups" for others. My thanks to Chuck, James, Jim, Paul, and Rocky in the men's group and Debbie L, Debbie T, Jan, Louise, Marge, and Sara in the women's group.

Your Best Life in Jesus' Easy Yoke is a completely updated and re-formatted version of the original. Whether you read it alone, with a friend, or in a group as originally intended, I pray it will be as groundbreaking for you as it's been for me and my friends.

May you be relaxed and productive in Jesus' easy yoke!

Bill Gaultiere

January 1st, 2016

The Apprentice Prayer

Many Christians today think that learning to be like Jesus is optional. Perhaps later they'll get more serious with God. We may believe in Christ yet have *whole areas of our life he's not part of.*

This was true for me in my late thirties. I was keeping my feet in two worlds: God's kingdom and my kingdom. I had lost the passion for Christ that I had as a young adult. I realized this one weekend in 2002 when Kristi and I were at John Eldredge's "Journey of Desire" conference. The Lord got hold of my heart and I began praying earnestly for Jesus to be my *First Love* again.

To stay close to the holy fire, I practiced disciplines like those that are featured in this book. Also, I met regularly with Ray Ortlund for spiritual mentoring and prayer over a number of years. I became a student of Dallas Willard, gleaning from his spiritual formation books and seminars and then meeting with him as I had done with Ray.

I wanted to learn from Jesus how to live my *whole life* in the Kingdom of God. I re-submitted and re-dedicated my life to Christ. I determined to live by Ray's heart-throbbing prayer: "Be all and only for Jesus!"[3] I determined to be a "true apprentice" to Christ (Matthew 10:42, MSG).

At the epicenter of this earth-shaking change was my prayer of devotion to Jesus that my friend Pastor Bucky Dennis dubbed "The Apprentice Prayer."[4] Most every morning for the first eight years of my renewal I offered this prayer from my heart. (My morning prayers to this day still draw on these themes.) I invite you to pray with me:

Jesus, I love you! Father, I adore you. Holy Spirit, I rely on you.

Lord Jesus, I seek to live as your apprentice in all that I do today. My life is your school for teaching me. I relinquish my agenda for this day and I submit myself to you and your kingdom purposes. In all things today I pray, "Your will, your way, your time."

Dear Father, I ask you to ordain the events of this day and use them to make me more like Jesus. I trust you, Sovereign Lord, that you won't let anything happen to my family or me today, *except that it passes through your loving hands.* So no matter what problems, hardships, or injustices I face today help me not to worry or get frustrated, but instead to relax in the yoke of your providence. Yes, today I will rejoice because I am in your eternal kingdom, you love me, and you are teaching me!

My Lord, I devote my whole self to you. *I want to be all and only for you, Jesus!* Today, I seek to love you with all my heart, all my soul, all my mind, all my strength, and all my relationships.[5]

Today, I depend on you, Holy Spirit, not my own resources. Help me to keep in step with you.

Today, I look to love others as you love me, dear God, blessing everyone I meet, even those who mistreat me.

Today, I'm ready to lead people to follow you, Jesus.

Amen.

Thousands of people, even whole churches, have prayed this prayer with me. Many have put it on their bathroom mirror, beside their bed, in their pocket, or in their Bible. They've prayed it every day for a year or more. With enthusiasm they've told me that God has used it to help them experience their own spiritual renewal.

I hope you'll join us in offering The Apprentice Prayer each morning. The upcoming chapters will provide further insight and application to it, helping you learn to *do all that you do in the easy yoke of apprenticeship to Christ.*

One

Come to Jesus

One day I was having lunch with Dallas Willard and he asked me, "If you had *one word* to describe Jesus what would it be?"

How would *you* answer that question? If you could only use *one word* to describe Jesus what would it be?

Words for Jesus started *running* through my mind and out my mouth: *Love... Compassion... Holy... Lord... Teacher... Risen... Healer...* (These are *all* good words to describe Jesus.)

As he so often did in my conversations with him, Dallas waited quietly for me to keep thinking. *He was unhurried.* I was drawn into his silent prayer.

Finally, I asked, "Dallas[6], what's your word for Jesus?"

He smiled, "Relaxed."[7]

Relaxed?

If anybody besides Dallas had said that I would've dismissed it. But he'd done so much to teach me to honor the supremacy of the Lord Jesus Christ and bring my life into the Kingdom of God. I'd read every book of his more than once and spent over two thousand hours listening to him speak.[8] I found his insights consistent with the Bible and transformational in real life.

Jesus is Relaxed and Fruitful

After that conversation I studied Jesus in the Gospels and found that in scene after scene he was indeed *at ease:*

- When it's time to launch his public ministry Jesus is *unhurried* and goes to the desert to pray for forty days (Mark 1:12-13).

- When his family tries to manipulate him in front of a crowd he *calmly sets a boundary* (Mark 3:31-34).

- When crowds interrupt his retreat he *patiently* feeds them (Mark 6:32-44).

- When he's in a small boat at sea and caught in a life-threatening storm he *naps* (Mark 4:37-38).

- When he sees loan sharks and hucksters turning his Father's house into a marketplace and taking advantage of the poor he *takes time* to weave a rope to drive them out (Mark 11:11, 12:15-17).

- When religious scholars gang up on him with trick questions he *speaks the truth in love* to them (Mark 12:13-17).

- When he's sweating drops of blood in the Garden he *finds comfort* in God as Abba (Mark 14:36).

- While being tortured to death he *lovingly ministers* to everyone around him, even his enemies (Luke 23:34, 43).

In all these difficult and important situations the Lord is *relaxed.*[9]

Wait a minute, I bet your thinking. *Jesus wasn't relaxed when he cleansed the temple! He wasn't calm in the garden or on the cross!*

Certainly, Jesus has some very *un*-relaxed emotions in these and other situations. Anguish, excruciating pain, overwhelming pressure, fear, anger, and grief certainly work against *feeling* relaxed. But the Master shows us that even in crisis or pain a mature person who is attuned to and aligned with God's presence can be calm, joyful, and loving.

Peace in Stress

The Easy Yoke of Jesus is not for an *easy life* — there's no such thing! Especially today in our 24 x 7 world. According to the World Health Organization stress is the health epidemic of the 21st century.

Kristi and I added an enormous stress to our full plates not quite two years after that lunch meeting with Dallas: we started

"Soul Shepherding, Inc." as a 501c3 nonprofit ministry to help pastors and leaders cultivate their intimacy with Jesus and strengthen their capacity to care for others. *We couldn't have done this without knowing Christ as relaxed under pressure.*

We faced many challenges that tempted us to fear and worry. Setting aside successful careers to launch a nonprofit ministry in the middle of the worst recession in decades. Fundraising. Leading an organization and a Board of Directors. Consulting for high profile Christian leaders.

How do you do what you don't know how to do? You need divine knowledge and power beyond your own abilities!

Rely on the risen Christ with you as your Leader and you'll *relax!*

For instance, in that same conversation with Dallas I told him I was going to lead a retreat for the staff of a megachurch. I'd led many retreats for smaller groups, but not for 150 leaders! I didn't know how to facilitate intimacy with Jesus for such a large group.

He remarked, "I hope you're not anxious about it."

I hesitated for a few moments. I *was* feeling stressed, but looking into Dallas' eyes I came back to my senses.

"No," I replied. *"Jesus is leading the retreat* and I'm assisting him. I just want to draw people to him."

"That's exactly right!" my mentor beamed.[10] I was thankful for God's "peace that passes understanding" (Philippians 4:6) — the *shalom* that is beyond anything we can figure out because it's from a hidden, heavenly source and it's obtained in ways that are contrary to the wisdom of our world. Indeed, the Lord helped me to remain in his peace-filled yoke as I led the retreat.

Easy-yoke is an oxymoron.

Relaxed, But Maybe Too Lax?

In Jesus' day a rabbi's teaching was called a yoke. The teaching-yoke of the religion scholars and priests was an endless list of laws, rules, traditions, and expectations that no one could measure up to.

But Jesus offered to free the people, including the religious leaders, from this deadly yoke of legalism. He opened his heart to anyone who would listen and offered his life-giving yoke of love:

> Come to me, all you who are weary and burdened, and I will give you rest. Take my yoke upon you and learn from me, for I am gentle and humble in heart, and you will find rest for your souls. For my yoke is easy and my burden is light (Matthew 11:28-30).

Let's soak in Jesus' invitation: "Come to me... Lay down your heavy burdens... Receive my gentle love... Rest deeply... Be easy as you work in my power..."

That's a God-blessed life! And the weary common people *thronged to Jesus* to experience it. Even some of the religious leaders accepted Jesus' wonderful teaching.

"This teaching on the easy yoke is just what I need to hear!" an Executive Pastor said to me. "I overwork and don't leave enough margin to rest in the Lord. But I wouldn't want my Youth Pastor to hear this — he's already *too lax* about his ministry responsibilities!"

I clarified, "Actually, Jesus isn't inviting us to slack off or even to go on a spiritual retreat — *he's offering to put a yoke on us!*"

Probably we want the "easy," but not the "yoke." Yokes are binding and they're for working hard!

A Lesson on Yokes

You probably haven't seen a yoke in awhile. Let's review the basics. The yoke that Jesus is referring to is a heavy wooden harness that fits over the shoulders of two oxen. It's used to attach them, neck to neck, and hitch up them up to a plow that they are to pull across a field to prepare it for planting a crop.

First the new ox needs to be "broken in." To train a young ox wise farmers are careful not to pair it with another young ox or an ox that's been poorly trained. Young oxen might be strong and energetic, but they don't know how to wear the yoke and they don't know how to pull the plow. They jerk and strain to try to get out of the yoke. They charge forward to rush to the end of the job, chaffing their necks and choking themselves. Or they try to wander off to graze in a meadow.

But if you take a young ox and pair it with a mature ox who has been well-trained then it learns. The lead ox shows the younger how to wear the yoke *loosely and lightly*. It pulls the brunt of the weight of the plow and leads the younger one to pull the plow slow and steady, step-by-step, straight ahead — without getting bruised or worn out.

Jesus is the mature ox we need. But sometimes I find myself *un-yoked* to the Sovereign Lord and *un-easy!* When Kristi sees me reverting to my old pattern of self-reliance and getting weighed down by my work she reminds me, "Bill, it's God's field, not yours! You don't have to plow the field all by yourself — he's inviting you to participate in His work." *Thank you Lord, this book is your project, not mine!*

Kristi needs my help too. Sometimes she sees "hard" disciplines that I or others are using and thinks she should follow suit, but I remind her, "Don't get in anybody's yoke but Jesus'. He custom fits his yoke to be a 'light burden' for you." It's the same for you reading these words. *The Savior adapts his yoke according to your needs — so don't compare yourself to other people!*

To be un-yoked to the Lord is an un-easy life!

Ravished For Jesus!

I was forty years old when I discovered the Gospel of Christ as an Easy Yoke and *the Lord inflamed my heart with his love!* I learned to live with the blessed awareness that the risen Christ is standing beside me, smiling and opening his arms to me!

This is true for you, *right now.*

"Come to me," the Radiant Son says to us. "Follow me and I will give you life — real life, my life in God, abundant and eternal living, more vitality than you could imagine, more joy than you can contain, the peace that you've always longed for."[11]

If only we would let Jesus *ravish our hearts!* If only we would appreciate the glorious gift of Christ crucified and risen. If only we would see that awaiting us right now is the opportunity of a lifetime: to be Jesus' apprentice, to bring our lives into his classroom, to make our world his kingdom, to shine his light to people all around us.

When we behold in our hearts the goodness and beauty of Christ then we *will* be captivated by him! We'll leave behind anything that distracts us. We'll lay down our burdens. We'll take his hand and follow him wherever he leads. Indeed, person after person in the New Testament *chased* after Christ.

People shouted out at the top of their lungs and made fools of themselves to get Jesus' attention. They pushed their way through crowds or crawled in the dirt and between people's legs to touch him. They walked across deserts, sat in the hot sun for hours and hours, and skipped meals to listen to him teach. They left their businesses and their families to follow him. They endured ridicule and abuse to be his disciples. They jumped out of trees, ripped the roofs off houses, and gave up their life savings to fall at his feet and worship him!

How will you give your heart afresh to Jesus? How will you step out of your comfort zone to grow in your apprenticeship to Christ the Lord?

We talk about "giving up everything to follow Jesus," but we need to start small — like giving up a little pride to lift our hands in worship or talk with a stranger while praying for a natural opportunity to bring the name of Jesus into the conversation.

A little thing I've done is to *literally skip with joy that I get to be one of Jesus' students!* Some people think I'm crazy. One day I got an email from one of the readers of our weekly Soul Shepherding Devotional email.[12] She wrote:

I like the way you want us to 'delight' in the Lord like a 'child,' as I've always felt this is the way God would love us to approach him. But I don't know if I would 'skip' like a child and then say, '*I am the disciple Jesus loves!*' I think my roommate just might call the 'men in the white coats' on me!

I replied: "Bring on the white coats! I'll be crazy for Jesus!"

The Triangle of Soul Transformation[13]

Jesus ministers the word of the Gospel to us: "Don't try to run your own life — you'll *ruin* it! God's glorious kingdom is available to you. I'm welcoming you into my Trinitarian society so put your confidence in me."[14]

Looking to Christ is the key that opens this portal to heaven. So we begin The Apprentice Prayer exclaiming, "Jesus, I love you! Father, I adore you. Holy Spirit, I rely on you." There are three general ways to look to the Word and Spirit of Jesus. These make up a triangle that summarizes Soul Shepherding's "Curriculum of Christlikeness," which is the basis of this book:

Triangle of Soul Transformation

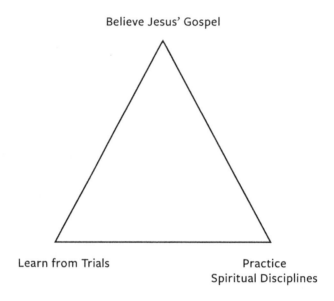

Believe Jesus' Gospel

Learn from Trials   Practice
                                        Spiritual Disciplines

1. Believe Jesus' Gospel

Each chapter in *Easy Yoke* will de-bunk a deceitful and damaging assumption held by most people. We'll shed the light of Christ on Satan's lies and our culture's foolishness. We'll *captivate* our minds and hearts on our precious Lord and the transforming truth of his Gospel: "Re-think your strategy for life because God's kingdom is open to you now" (Matthew 4:19, paraphrased).[15]

Studying and meditating on the Bible, especially the Gospels, is essential for our spiritual formation in Christlikeness. We all have been "conformed to the pattern of this world" and by God's mercy need to "be transformed by the renewing of our minds" in Scripture (Romans 12:1-2). It is singularly *the life of Jesus Christ —* and learning to participate in his life by his Spirit of grace — that unleashes the goodness and power of the Bible to renew our minds. So each chapter will look at an aspect of Jesus' holy and wholesome character which he offers to us.

2. Learn from Trials

We will also focus on a common stress-related problem in each chapter. Rather than directly seeking relief from anxiety and distress (which doesn't work), you'll be encouraged to seek God and his heavenly kingdom in the middle of your daily life difficulties (Matthew 6:33). Seeing our trials as tests of our character and accepting them as *learning opportunities* is crucial to experiencing enduring joy in God (James 1:2-6). To keep trusting Christ and to prevail over our problems we need to be vulnerable with friends who give empathy and grace (John 16:33; James 5:16).

Each of us needs to be part of a community of apprentices to Jesus in order to become more like him, which is why *Easy Yoke* is meant to be shared among sacred companions. We need to support and care for one another in order to persevere and grow through the difficulties of our lives.

3. Practice Spiritual Disciplines

Paul says, "Train yourself to be godly" (1 Timothy 4:7). He's urging his young assistant pastor to use disciplines to grow in Christly character (developing habits of love). We need to use a variety of these exercises under the leadership of the Holy Spirit in order to apply the gospel of grace to our daily lives. We do these *experimentally,* adjusting what we do and how we do it based on what is most helpful for our healing and growth in Christ.

For instance, in the Sermon on the Mount Jesus introduces three qualities of genuine righteousness: generosity, prayerfulness, and self-denial. To help us become this kind of person there are related disciplines that we can practice: giving/ service, praying Scripture (especially the Lord's Prayer), and fasting (Matthew 6:1-18).

At the end of each chapter of *Easy Yoke* there is a Spiritual Experiment aimed at de-stressing in Jesus' easy yoke. You'll be guided to make quiet space to engage with God through praying

Scripture. Then you'll be encouraged to share your experiences and insights with friends on the journey by responding to the Soul Talk questions.

It's a "Golden Triangle"

The Triangle of Soul Transformation is about "being transformed into [Christ's] image with ever-increasing glory, which comes from the Lord, who is the Spirit" (2 Corinthians 3:18). We're seeking to *internalize* and *imitate* Christ Jesus with our true self and total personality.[16]

This triangle is "golden" in that it's three priorities integrate to work together: you can't do one well without also doing the other two, as each feeds into the others. It's best to begin at the top with the Gospel, but in practice you can "start" anywhere on the triangle and move in any direction as long as you keep the three priorities together and balanced.

For instance, our belief in Christ and his Gospel (top corner) is tested in trials which motivate us to seek support from other people (left corner). To overcome our sin and stress and to be more loving we need to practice disciplines for life in the Spirit (right corner). These learning experiences lead us to worship the the Lord or to re-think our faith-strategy for life (top corner).

Experiment

Lectio Divina

In the 6th Century Benedict of Nursia in Italy taught the monks who followed Christ with him to meditate on Bible passages using a process he called "Lectio Divina" (Latin for "Divine Reading.") In the centuries since then, Benedictines and others have refined his approach. The method that Kristi and I learned is adapted from the Benedictine monks at Saint Andrews Abbey in Valyermo, CA.

Our method of Lectio Divina is especially focused on listening to Scripture with our heart. It's different than Bible study, but complementary to it. Instead of studying and analyzing the text (which we do at another time), we enter into the passage *experientially,* feeling our emotions and needs, listening to the Holy Spirit speak into our daily life, and resting in God's grace. In our Soul Shepherding ministry we've found it very helpful to share this contemplative and personal experience of the Word with spiritual direction clients, small groups, and ministry teams.[17]

I'd like to lead you in Lectio Divina on our Master's easy yoke teaching in Matthew 11:25-30 from *The Message* version. This Scripture meditation will be carried into each chapter of *Easy Yoke.*[18] We'll discover many fresh insights and applications for experiencing and sharing with others the Lord's life-giving rhythms of grace!

Imagine that you and some friends are in a Soul Shepherding group with me following our Lectio Divina Guide for "Step Into Jesus' Easy Yoke."[19] It's a confidential group and as the leader I ask everyone to follow my prompts for the pacing of each element and what to do next. (To do this meditation on your own now you'll want to allow about thirty minutes. Later you may want to share this with a friend or small group in which case you'll want to allow more time.)

Lectio Divina Process (Repeated for Three Readings)

1. Read the Scripture passage ("Lectio")

2. Reflect on the focus question below ("Meditatio")

3. Respond in quiet prayer/journaling ("Oratio")

4. Rest in God's invitation for you, then pray/share out loud if you want ("Contemplatio")

Introduction/Context of Passage

Jesus has just denounced the cities where he did most of his miracles because they did not turn from their sins and put their trust in him as Lord and Savior. He's pronouncing God's judgment on those cities when *suddenly he stops to pray.* Then he changes his tone to tenderness and invites the people to join the easy yoke of his intimacy with the Father.

Scripture Reading

Three group members take turns reading the passage out loud. For each reading there is a focus question to guide the time of prayerful listening with optional journaling.

Matthew 11:25-30 (*The Message*)[20]

> Abruptly Jesus broke into prayer: "Thank you, Father, Lord of heaven and earth. You've concealed your ways from sophisticates and know-it-alls, but spelled them out clearly to ordinary people [even little children]. Yes, Father, that's the way you like to work."

> Jesus resumed talking to the people, but now tenderly. "The Father has given me all these things to do and say. This is a unique Father-Son operation, coming out of Father and Son intimacies and knowledge. No one knows the Son the way the Father does, nor the Father the way the Son does. But I'm not keeping it to myself; I'm ready to go over it line by line with anyone willing to listen.

"Are you tired? Worn out? Burned out on religion? Come to me. Get away with me and you'll recover your life. I'll show you how to take a real rest. [Take my yoke upon you for I am gentle and humble in heart and we'll pull the plow across the field together.] Walk with me and work with me — watch how I do it. Learn the unforced rhythms of grace [that go with my easy yoke]. I won't lay anything heavy or ill-fitting on you. Keep company with me and you'll learn to live freely and lightly."

Focus Questions for Prayer (With Space For Journaling)

1. *1st Reading:* What is one word or phrase the Holy Spirit impresses on you? Meditate on that.

2. *2nd Reading.* Enter into the Scripture passage. What do you feel? What specific situation in your life today relates? Write down a prayer or pray quietly.

3. *3rd Reading.* What is God's personal invitation for you from the Scripture? You can write down what God may be saying to you or a prayer of thanks. Or rest quietly in God.

A Breath Prayer From the Bible

Near the end of each chapter in *Easy Yoke* there is a "Breath Prayer." This is not a New Age practice. It goes back to the Christian Fathers and Mothers of the third century who lived in the desert and learned to pray without ceasing using the Jesus

Prayer: "Lord Jesus Christ, have mercy on me." (We'll re-visit the Jesus Prayer later.)

A few Christians criticize Breath Prayers as being the "vain repetitions" of pagans that Jesus told us to avoid (Matthew 6:7). But he was referring to meaningless babbling, not savoring a verse of holy Scripture! In the Bible itself the Psalmist often directs us to repeat short prayers of the heart like, "Your love endures forever" (e.g., Psalm 136). Similarly, in the Psalter we often take a "Selah" ("say-lah") of quiet reflection during the singing of a Psalm. (We'll explore Selah in Chapter Six.)

The breathing prayers that I do are from the Bible and I do them as a simple and practical way to take my meditation on God's word from my mind into my physical being and all the way down into my heart. Like raising my hands in worship or kneeling in prayer, I'm purposefully using my body to engage personally with the Lord.[21]

The first Breath Prayer I'd like to share with you will help foster your apprenticeship to Christ Jesus and your experience of his peace. It's just six words long, but to write it took me *two months!* I had been praying Psalm 20 and was particularly drawn to verse seven: "Some trust in chariots and some trust in horses, but we trust in the name of the Lord our God." As I ruminated on this like a cow chewing it's cud it reminded me of our Lord saying, "My yoke is easy."

I asked the Holy Spirit to help me write a simple and heartfelt breathing prayer that I could carry with me throughout a day. I kept coming back to this until a couple of months later I finally came up with: "In Jesus' name... Not my strain." (See Psalm 20:7.)

In other words, we're praying: "Jesus, I trust you and rely on you alone... Not what I can achieve or who I can please."

Let's try this breathing prayer now. *How sweet it is to appreciate the precious and powerful name of our Lord and Savior Jesus Christ!* This is an opportunity to release our worries and our burdens to the Lord and find peace in him. Inhaling and exhaling this little prayer is as easy as it is delightful! Try it this way:

- Breathe in as you pray with a whisper or thought: "In Jesus' name..."
- In the same way, breathe out: "Not my strain..."
- Repeat this a number of times...

Apprenticeship to Jesus is total reliance on his name and letting go of all strain.

Training for Breathing and Praying God's Word

To draw all the sweetness and strength from this prayer you need to keep practicing it so that it's Biblical content and rhythms begin to *live in your body as an unconscious habit.* You can train your mind, body, and heart with these steps:

1. Do some deep breathing

When you're stressed, hurried, or under pressure you're breathing tends to become shallow, which takes you out of enjoying God in the moment. Practice breathing in deep... Holding your breath... And breathing out slowly... You may want to inhale through your nose and exhale through your mouth... Relax...

2. Make your breathing a prayer

Train your mind to associate inhaling with receiving a gift of grace from God and exhaling with letting go of (or renouncing) strain, anxiety, anger, or self-condemnation. Your pattern of breathing is becoming a prayer that is so deep in you that it has *unconscious* (bodily) meaning. You're learning to Breathe in tandem with the Holy Spirit.

3. *Pray Scripture*

Now add the words to the breathing rhythm. Inhale, "In Jesus' name..." Exhale, "Not my strain..." Continue with this until you feel connected to the Prince of Peace.

4. *Watch and pray*

Jesus teaches the importance of preparing for temptations and trials (Matthew 26:41). Perhaps you're struggling with finances, a conflict, or a challenge... Ask God to help you trust him in that situation as you breathe: "In Jesus' name... Not my strain..." Keep praying this, while visualizing your circumstance, until you can shift from stress to peace...

Soul Talk

At the end of each chapter of *Easy Yoke* you'll have opportunity to reflect and pray on a few questions. You may want to write your responses down in your journal to prepare you to share with your friends.

1. What was your experience with The Apprentice Prayer?

2. Which Gospel example of Jesus being relaxed under pressure is especially helpful to you? Why?

3. What are your thoughts about how The Triangle of Soul Transformation can instruct your path of growth in Christ?

4. How did it feel to do the breathing prayer, "In Jesus' name... Not my strain"?

Two

In Jesus' Non-Anxious Yoke

In 2009 I won a medal for finishing the "Surf City" marathon in Huntington Beach, CA. I ran 26.2 miles in under 4 hours. It was the fifth marathon I'd completed and it was actually my slowest one, but it might be the one I'm the most proud of because I did it at 46 years old. The other four I did in the physical prime of my life, between ages 17 and 21.

You're probably thinking to yourself: "Running 26.2 miles is too hard!"

That's how many people feel about the Christian life. "The road is really narrow and difficult," we say. But when Jesus contrasted the narrow and broad roads his point was actually *the opposite!* The broad road leads to destruction that keeps getting worse all the way into eternity. The narrow road leads to life that keeps getting better and better. Jesus is concerned that we not miss out on the best way of life (Matthew 7:13-14).

Yes, there is a cost of discipleship. We give up sinful pleasures. We endure many trials. We're persecuted for our faith in Christ. Satan and his demons attack us.

But *the cost of non-discipleship is actually much more!* Not only in eternity but also in this life, though it often doesn't look like it based on *outward appearances*. Compare the long-term effects of addiction to those of self-control and moderation, or chronic lying to honesty. Clearly, "virtue is its own reward" is a true saying. So Paul teaches us the law of sowing and reaping and urges, "Let us not become weary in doing good, for at the proper time we will reap a harvest if we do not give up" (Galatians 6:9).

Jesus is being most sincere when he motions to us, "Come to me... My yoke is easy and my burden is light." Walking in Jesus' rhythms of grace doesn't eliminate our stress (difficult or challenging situations), but it helps us *not to internalize stress and become anxious*. Living freely and lightly in the Spirit of Jesus doesn't mean we won't experience loss and disappointment, but it helps us *not be weighed down with depression*. Intimacy with Jesus and sharing in his work are so delightful, so honoring, and so encouraging that all of life, including the hard and painful parts, *can* be filled with grace and peace.

"Try Harder!"

Most people think that to be successful in anything they need to try really hard. Most of my life I've thought that way. We say to one another and to ourselves things like...

* "If at first you don't succeed, try, try, and try again."

* "It's up to me to make it happen."

* "I have to take control of the situation."

* "I need to get a grip on my emotions."

* "Life is hard."

Are these true statements? Is this God's wisdom for you and I to live by? In life, is God urging us: "C'mon. Try harder!"?

No. They may be half true, but ultimately they are *false belief systems*. Imagine trying to finish a marathon just by trying hard! You're determined to run 26.2 miles without stopping or even walking — even though you haven't run one mile in years. But you're motivated! You're going to run hard! You're going to push yourself to keep running no matter how tired and sore you get!

Your body and my body won't let us run long distances without building up to it over time. It doesn't matter how much will power we exert. If we try to force ourselves to run farther or faster than our capacity then we'll run out of breath or be in too much pain to continue. And if we somehow keep making ourselves run anyway then eventually we'll start throwing up, get injured, or collapse in exhaustion.

There is no doubt that effort is required to run a marathon, but it is *not sufficient*. The spiritual life works the same way. You can't sustain godly behavior by telling yourself that you must do what you should. You've told yourself things like, "Be kind... Don't get stressed... Don't get angry... I need to pray more..."

You've tried and tried harder to do what you should and sometimes you've succeeded (which usually leads to pride) but then eventually you weren't able to sustain your good behavior — discouraged, you may have given up trying altogether.

Living in Jesus' non-anxious yoke begins
with understanding our stress points.

The religious Scribes and Pharisees in Jesus' day tried hard to do what they should. Theirs was a legalistic righteousness that was depressing, destructive, and deadly. Jesus called them "whitewashed tombstones" — on the outside they were clean, manicured, and surrounded by flowers, but inside they were full or rotting flesh and dead bones (Matthew 23:27-28). He said that our righteousness must go far beyond theirs (be a totally different kind!) if we want to enter the Kingdom of God (Matthew 5:20).

Do You Have A-N-X-I-E-T-Y?

The "try harder" mentality leads to anxiety. Let's see how you're doing with anxiety. Try my screening test to identify any symptoms of A-N-X-I-E-T-Y that you may struggle with. Each of the seven categories of anxious symptoms has two or more related questions. Answer each question with yes or no, meaning it's "mostly true" or "mostly not true" of you. Then underline your yes responses.

- *A gitated.* Are you easily frustrated? Do people irritate or upset you? Do you lose your temper often?

- *N ot sleeping/relaxing.* Are you having trouble getting to sleep or staying asleep? Do you often wake up and not feel rested? Is it hard for you to be still and relax?

- *X fears.* Do you have any fears that you accommodate by avoiding situations? Are you afraid of social situations, interpersonal conflict, rejection, failure, public speaking, leaving home, airplanes, spiders, knives?

- *I n your body.* Have you been experiencing shortness of breath, heart palpitations, tightness in your chest, discomfort in your stomach or bowels, headaches, twitching, shaking hands, sweaty palms, or tingling?

- *E scalating worries.* Are you worried about problems you're facing? Do you keep thinking over and over about your stress? Do your thoughts race out of control?

- *T raumas relived.* Does your mind keep re-experiencing an upsetting event(s)? Are you having nightmares?

- *Y es all the time.* Do you feel pressured to say yes to accommodate other people? Satisfy your perfectionism? Give into compulsive desires that won't go away?

If you have yes responses in three or more categories (or any yes answers that are disruptive for you) it suggests that anxiety may be shutting you off from God's peace, draining your energy, diminishing your effectiveness, or distracting you from opportunities to love God and the people around you.

If you keep internalizing stress anxiety gets into your body and it takes time to get it out!

Jen's Quivering Lip

Jen[22] sought my help when she couldn't get her lip to stop quivering with anxiety when she talked. This embarrassed her socially and it became a problem for her in her job because as the Women's Ministries Director in her church she often had to speak in front of audiences. She knew that she was anxious about her lip and what people were thinking about her, but she didn't know that she had a problem with *trying to control things.*

In everything she did Jen tried to do better. She wore the latest fashions and got her hair professionally styled every few weeks. She prided herself in making healthy meals for her family and being involved in her kids' lives. And after she put her kids to bed she stayed up late preparing the weekly Bible Study for working mothers which she led in her church.

Sometimes Jen's husband got frustrated with her that she didn't relax more and didn't have more time to go to shows, take bike rides to the beach, and do the things that they had enjoyed before having kids. But she always reassured him that things would get better when the kids were older.

Everyone who looked at Jen's life, including Jen, thought she had the perfect life. But Jen's quivering lip wouldn't stop. She found herself tightening her lips to try to get them to stop trembling. She was losing her smile! She was becoming more and more self-conscious and anxious about the talks she gave at church and the small group she led in her home.

The harder Jen tried to keep up her ideal, put-together image, the more anxious she became. Hiding her "flaw" wasn't working.

Anxiety is a Control Problem

You may not have an obvious anxiety symptom, but probably there are times that you internalize stress and worry. As we'll discuss further in Chapter Three, stress (as in outward changes, challenges, and responsibilities) is part of life and in moderation it's good because it activates us. *But to convert stress into internal anxiety is a problem.* Chronic anxiety can cause us sickness and disease and it wears down both us and our loved ones. So Paul says,

> Do not be anxious about anything, but in every situation, by prayer and petition, with thanksgiving, present your requests to God. And the peace of God, which transcends all understanding, will guard your hearts and your minds in Christ Jesus (Philippians 4:6-7).

That may seem like Paul is telling us to deny our emotional distress, but actually it's the *opposite!* In effect Paul is saying, "When you start to feel anxious reflect on your underlying emotions, ask God for what you need, and thank him for what he's doing. Then his peace will guard your heart."

Like a wise psychologist, Paul understood that anxiety is a *secondary emotion* that we feel when we don't trust God with our primary emotions of fear, anger, or grief but instead we try to control those feelings through repression and denial.

Francis de Sales, he 16th century Jesuit spiritual director and Frenchman, described the control issues (the "try harder" script) that cause the "unregulated desire" of anxiety.

> Anxiety arises from an unregulated desire to be delivered from a pressing [problem], or to obtain some hoped-for good... Birds that are captured in nets and snares become inextricably entangled therein, because they flutter and struggle so much. Therefore... strive above all else to keep a calm, restful spirit; steady your judgment and will, and then go quietly and easily [out of your snare]...

> When you are conscious that you are growing anxious, commend yourself to God, and resolve steadfastly not to take any steps whatever to obtain the result you desire, until your disturbed state of mind is altogether quieted... so as to act rather from reason than impulse.

> If you can lay your anxiety before your spiritual guide, or at least before some trusty and devout friend, you may be

sure that you will find great solace. The heart finds relief in telling its troubles to another.[23]

In sum, to be anxious is like being a bird that's caught in a net and flutters about wildly trying to get free, rather than relaxing and simply walking through a hole in the net! When we're anxious we're *trying too hard to get what we want:* feel admired, be strong, look successful, and not have any vulnerable emotions! But freedom comes in the opposite direction. We need to be aware of our personal emotions and needs, receive the empathy that calms us down, and learn to rely on God's grace one day at a time.

Keep receiving empathy and you won't suffer from chronic anxiety.

It's Astonishing How Relaxed Jesus Was!

In Chapter 1 we were surprised to see Jesus as relaxed. Let's connect further with the Lord's *non-anxious presence* — this is the key to lasting peace!

Jesus had far and away the most important and dangerous human mission and he had to wait eighteen years to begin working on it and then he had just three years (of public ministry) to fulfill it. And yet Jesus was *relaxed!*

Our Master needed to convince a large number people that although he was a human being like them he was also the unique Son of God. His followers needed to be so confident in him that they'd be willing to suffer and die for him. And yet Jesus was *relaxed!*

Jesus had to leave cities full of people that needed more ministry from him (Matthew 13:58). And yet Jesus was *relaxed!*

Jesus' family rejected him and his message (Luke 4:28-30, Mark 3:20, 31-34). Many of his disciples deserted him (John 6:66). Even his faithful followers didn't really understand who he was right up through his death (Mark 8:31-33). And yet Jesus was *relaxed!*

Our Lord had no rest from being stressed by Satan, demons, wicked kings, contemptuous Pharisees, wealthy snobs, raging mobs, seductive prostitutes, flattering sycophants, party animals, and fickle friends. And yet Jesus was *relaxed!*

Jesus was tempted to sin in all the same ways that we are (Hebrews 2:18). And he experienced all of our weaknesses and painful emotions (Hebrews 4:15, 5:2). And yet Jesus was relaxed!

The fate of all humankind for all times depended on the Messiah successfully completing his Gospel mission! And yet Jesus was *relaxed!*

Jesus was crucified on a cross; he was tortured by enemies, abandoned by friends, insulted by passers by; he became a sin offering for us. And yet Jesus was *relaxed!* (Even with some unrelaxed emotions, as we said earlier on p. 4.)

When I have big responsibilities I sometimes start taking charge to make things happen. When I have lots to do I tend to hurry. When I am stressed anxious feelings may grip me. When I am criticized or rejected I might react by feeling bad about myself or getting angry. When I am in terrible pain I have difficulty being loving to others.

How did Jesus remain at peace when he was under overwhelming stress and pain? How can you or I be more at ease? Our Savior practiced what he preached! His holiness wasn't "automatic" because he was the Son of God. He chose to live in the same grace-yoke that he offers to us. He was the first disciple; he apprenticed himself to the Father as a child and throughout his life, learning to live out the things he would later teach us.

It's important for us to appreciate the mysterious reality that the Son of God, our sinless Lord, "grew" (Luke 2:52); he "learned" (Hebrews 5:8) many things about living a divine life in a human body, like how to:

- Continually submit to God's will, only saying and doing what was in concert with his Father (John 6:38, 12:50).

- Pray without ceasing (John 11:42, 1 Thessalonians 5:17).

- Remain so dependent upon the Holy Spirit as to be filled with his presence and power without limit (John 3:34).

- Bless those that cursed him (Luke 22:34).

Being relaxed in his Abba Father's arms of love — even when stressed, in pain, or being mistreated by enemies — is what enabled Jesus to love others perfectly and to fulfill all the lofty words that we use to describe him.

Relaxing in Jesus' Easy Yoke

For most of my life if you had one word to describe me you would never have used the word "relaxed!" "Intense," yes! "Stressed," probably. "Anxious," maybe. Perhaps it's because "Will I am" means "Determined!"

Prior to my renewal when I had big responsibilities I would always try hard and then *try harder.* When I was stressed by situations I'd feel overwhelmed or anxious. When I had problems I worried. When I was challenged I strained to make things turn out right. When people looked at me I tried to show them my ideal self. I always pressured myself to do what seemed best.

I wasn't in the yoke of the Lord's sovereignty. To be sure, with all my heart I believed that Christ was Lord and I wanted him to be in charge of everything that concerned me, but I hadn't adequately trained my *body* to stay in that yoke so I missed out on its ease and effectiveness.

"You gotta serve somebody," Bob Dylan sings.[24] You gotta yoke yourself to someone or something. You can't live without being yoked or attached to someone or something. This is what Jesus is saying in Matthew 11. His analogy is that we're all like oxen wearing a yoke. The question is what are we yoked to? Where are we placing our affections?

To a large extent, as a young man I was serving the idol of success. Others yoke themselves to pleasing a spouse, engaging in gossip, pornography, getting hooked on fantasy sports, or showing the world of Facebook how perfect their life is.

Eventually these are proved to be unsatisfying yokes. *The only joyful yokes are those that go with intimacy with Jesus.* When we're truly bonded to the Lord then all our other desires and endeavors are rightly ordered as expressions of our love for God. Attached to Christ we're set free and no longer "burdened by a yoke of slavery" (Galatians 5:1).

The yoke of sin is *much harder*
than the yoke of Christ.

But Jesus' yoke is a grace-yoke! Listen to his Easy Yoke Gospel:

Come to me. I want to help you to carry your burdens. Don't pull that heavy load in your own strength – enter into the harness with me. Let me show you how to pull the plow across the field and get the work done in a good and relaxed way. Walk with me and work with me. Look straight ahead and keep in cadence with me. We'll step together easily and lightly. We'll smile in the Father's love as we bless people in need.[25]

Grace is Not Passive

The "Father and Son intimacies and knowledge" with their "unforced rhythms of grace" are for you too! But *God's grace is not a passive thing.*

Tragically, in order to stay clear of works religion many Christians today end up being *paralyzed by grace!*[26] We think that as people of faith all we need to do is to go to church and have good doctrine or read the Bible and say our prayers. But doing just these standard activities, as we typically understand them, does not reliably transform people to be more like Jesus Christ. This is obvious when we look at the character of the average "Christian" in America. The Holy Spirit doesn't zap people into Christlikeness through inspiring sermons! God does not leap off the pages of the Bible and make people be loving disciples of Jesus!

Commonly we say that grace is "unmerited favor." That's true, but it doesn't tell us where grace is nor how it relates to our life today. We tend to limit God's grace to our need for forgiveness of our sins so we can go to heaven when we die. Of course, that is essential! But grace is more than that — *it's for all of life!*

Rely on God's grace to be energized and activated to love others in Jesus' name.

Grace is God acting in our lives generously and powerfully to do what we cannot do on our own. God acts and we respond. God's hand reaches out to us and we take hold. The Lord leads us and we follow him. It's up to us to interact with and rely upon God's favor and mercy in all that we do. Just as much as its true that, "Apart from Jesus you can do nothing" (John 15:5, paraphrase) so also its true that, "If you do nothing it will be apart from Jesus."

We need to understand that grace is not opposed to effort; it's opposed to *earning.* Earning is an attitude of pride and self-sufficiency, but effort has to do with taking appropriate action. Jesus teaches that to get into his grace-yoke we need to learn from him by walking with him and working with him. Remember his analogy is that we're in a yoke walking in stride together as we pull a plow across a field.

Being active in God's grace may seem like a contradiction to salvation by faith alone, but its not. Peter tells us to "Grow in the grace and knowledge of our Lord and Savior Jesus Christ" (2 Peter 3:18). And similarly the writer to Hebrews teaches us to "Make every effort to enter [God's] rest" (Hebrews 4:11).

Instead of trying harder and pushing to make things happen for ourselves we can learn to put our effort into relying on *Christ with us,* listening to him, and following his lead step-by-step. This is the Good News Gospel! This is the truth we can know through interacting with the grace of Christ and thereby be set free (John 8:32) from the burdensome cycle of trying hard... Feeling guilty... Trying harder... Getting exhausted and discouraged...

As a disciple of the Father Jesus learned the easy yoke life and teaches it to us.

Don't Try, Train[27]

Running the marathon was actually relatively easy for me (except for the last six miles!) because I didn't just try — I *trained.* I became a marathon runner *on the inside* — in my body and my mindset — so that in the race I'd be ready.

Every Saturday morning for months before the race I did a long run. I started with a four-mile run that goes alongside the two lakes near my home. Then each week I went a little farther, building up to a 20 mile-long run in the hills. I also did other running and worked out with weights.

The secret to any training program is *indirection.* You can't improve or grow directly by will power. Instead you do what you can do and with repetition over time you are gradually empowered to do what you could not do at the start. By disciplining yourself to practice your exercises you get stronger and better and are able to do more with less strain.[28]

It's because of my training that I was able to enjoy running the 26.2-mile race. What a thrill it was to run on paths lined with people cheering me on as I made my way through parks and along the ocean. And then what a joy it was to cross the finish line with Kristi, our three kids, my dad, and thousands of other people cheering for me!

What I enjoyed most about my marathon was the time to be quiet, meditate on Scripture, and to pray. *I like to run with Jesus!* He is the Champion of Psalm 19 who is rejoicing to run his course in the heavens all around me (v 5). So as I run my life's race I fix my eyes on Jesus. I converse with him. I follow him. He is the author and perfecter of my faith (Hebrews 12:2).

The Apostle Paul was apparently a fan of the Olympic games and he used this analogy to teach us to discipline ourselves to grow in the grace of Christ:

> Do you not know that in a race all the runners run, but only one gets the prize? Run in such a way as to get the prize.

> Everyone who competes in the games goes into strict training. They do it to get a crown that will not last; but we do it to get a crown that will last forever. Therefore I do not run like a man running aimlessly; I do not fight like a man beating the air. No, I beat my body and make it my slave so that after I have preached to others, I myself will not be disqualified for the prize (1 Corinthians 9:24-27, MSG).

> Exercise daily in God — no spiritual flabbiness please! (1 Timothy 4:7, MSG).

Paul lived this way so that even when he was mistreated and suffering in jail he sung out: "Rejoice always! Again I say rejoice!" (Philippians 4:4).

The 1924 Olympic runner Eric Liddell, who was depicted in the movie "Chariots of Fire," demonstrates Paul's joyful spirit under stress. As he sprints around the track he holds a Scripture on a piece of paper, tilts his head back to look up to heaven, flails his arms exuberantly, and laughs with a wide open mouth! That's great form! He says to himself and to the world: *"God made me for a purpose. He made me fast! And when I run I feel his pleasure!"*

When do you feel God's pleasure?

O dear friends, let's approach our life with Christ like Eric Liddell ran! We begin by asking the Lord Jesus Christ to be our Life Coach. We do spiritual "work outs" with him. He helps us to grow in his grace and become stronger in love by designing a training routine that is specially suited for our individual needs, abilities, and personality. He guides us and encourages as we do our exercises.

Then when we leave the gym he accompanies us and shows us how to do all that we're doing in his unforced rhythms of grace, relaxed in his love, and free of anxiety.

Jen Was Released From Anxiety

In counseling Jen talked with me about the anxious situations she'd experienced and I helped her to get under the surface to express her deeper emotions: fears about what people thought about her, pressures she put on herself to be a successful, anger at people, embarrassment and shame over her weaknesses. By bringing her formerly repressed emotions into a relationship of care she more deeply experienced God's unconditional love and perfect peace.

Another key for Jen was learning how to abandon outcomes to God. For instance, in the past she worried about her lip quivering or not giving a great presentation; she was afraid to be embarrassed in front of people. Instead she learned to accept that she couldn't control results and trying to do so only made her anxiety worse, which made her lip more likely to quiver! Releasing to God her fear and her public image greatly diminished her worry.

These are some ways that Jen trained her body, mind, and whole being to be ruled by the peace of Christ, not anxiety (Colossians 3:15). Eventually her body calmed down and her lip quivered less often.

Experiment

Abandoning Outcomes to God

As we've said, living by grace requires training. To become the kind of person who easily and routinely walks in the character and power of Christ you need to practice a wise regimen of disciplines for the spiritual life as "means of grace."[29] (This is the third corner of the Triangle of Soul Transformation.) Submission to God — getting in the yoke with Christ — is itself a discipline.

Jesus' yoke is easy, but getting into it and staying in it are *not* easy!

Yielding to God in all that we do is the way into the humble and anxiety-free yoke of Jesus. "The Father has given me all these things to do and say." By living in submission to God, the Scriptures, and other people, under Christ we'll grow in our experience of true peace, power, freedom, and love for others.

Richard Foster says submission is "the ability to lay down the terrible burden of always needing to get our own way... If we could only see that most things in life are not major issues, then we could hold them lightly."[30]

Jesus Lived in Submission

Perhaps the most astonishing aspect of Jesus' life on earth is that *as the Sovereign Lord he himself lived by the discipline of submission!* Throughout the Gospels we see Jesus resisting temptations to make things happen for himself or get people to do what he wanted. Instead he yields himself to the Father and discerns God's will in the midst of his circumstances.

Jesus Christ is the Lord God, co-equal with Father God and Parakletos God in the Trinity, and yet he chose to live his life on earth in subjection to God in all things, at all times. He chose to die on a cross and entrust his spirit to his Father in the heavens. This was the secret of his supernatural life!

Frank Laubach, a great evangelical missionary to Muslims and spiritual writer of the 20th Century, noted that the Apostle John indicates in his Gospel that Jesus was acting "under God's orders" *47 times!* John records Jesus saying things like: "I have come down from heaven not to do my will but to do the will of him who sent me... Whatever I say is just what the Father has told me to say" (John 6:38, 12:50).

Often Jesus let circumstances unfold; then he discerned and acted with God.

Jesus is the Living Word who spoke the Scriptures into existence and yet he lived in humble obedience to those very Scriptures! Again and again we read in the gospels that Jesus said and did certain things "so that the Scripture would be fulfilled."[31] He discovered his identity, lived out his life story, and made his every decision according to the written Word.

At times the King of kings and Lord of lords even submitted himself to the people he created! (Of course, he only did this as unto God.) Jesus confined himself to human flesh, was born in a stable and laid in an animal feeding trough, obeyed his parents, completed carpentry jobs for customers, submitted to John's baptism, paid taxes, performed menial servant duties, asked his disciples for help, surrendered to soldiers, subjected himself to illegal trials, yielded to Pilate's verdict, capitulated to the cross, and handed over his mission to his "little-faith" disciples.

If Jesus Christ, our Lord and Savior, lived in submission to God in all things then how could we do anything less?

How to Abandon Outcomes to God

To become a Christian means we're submitting our heart to God. But how do we live out that surrender in our daily lives?

Dallas Willard taught me to cultivate submission to the Lord in my spirit and body by practicing the discipline of "abandoning outcomes to God."[32] This concept makes submission to God concrete so we can apply it to our opportunities and challenges. It has helped me, and many people like Jen that I've talked with, to get in Jesus' yoke and grow in his peace.

Everyday there are things that we want, situations in our relationships, work, ministry, or projects that we'd like to have turn out a certain way, which, of course, is natural. But *pushing for a certain outcome is contrary to Jesus' easy yoke.* It's helpful to identify a situation to practice denying yourself what you want in order to submit to God's sovereign leading. Instead of trying to make things happen the way you want in that circumstance you *let go* of your agenda and entrust the results to God.

"Let go and let God" is a good saying if it means, "Submit to Christ and follow his leading." But often it's misunderstood to encourage a "laissez faire" attitude of passivity and disinterest along the lines of, "It doesn't really matter and there is nothing I can do." Abandoning outcomes to God is *an alert and vigorous process* of anticipating situations, praying about them, and being responsible to do what needs to be done — *while putting confidence in God to direct the outcomes.*

The Apprentice Prayer helps us to let go of control to God and follow his lead: Sovereign Lord, "I relinquish my agenda for this day and I submit myself to you and your kingdom purposes. In all situations I abandon outcomes to you, praying, 'Your will, your way, your time.'"

To abandon outcomes to God and enjoy his peace pray, "Your will, your way, your time."

To further make our submission to God practical it's helpful if we submit to a person *as unto Christ*. As John says in his epistle, "How can you love your unseen God if you don't love your brother or sister right in front of your eyes?" (1 John 4:20, paraphrased). As we trust godly people we cultivate an attitude of surrendering to Christ and his kingdom. Then you can draw your peace and power from the pierced hands in your midst.

Let's consider some typical situations in which you can replace worry or strain with abandoning outcomes to God. It'd be helpful to pick one or two to practice this week!

1. Wait and pray before acting.

When you have an opportunity wait on God before pursuing it. Or in a situation that you need to give leadership pause before you act. First, pray the line from The Apprentice Prayer: "Lord, your will, your way, your time." Also, you might ask for guidance from a friend. Be open to God re-directing you. Accept that you may "miss out" by not hurrying. It's okay! You can still enjoy and be shaped by God's loving presence!

2. Prepare for possible disappointment.

Consider that you may not succeed or someone may not be pleased. Pray to leave the results in God's hands. Of course, do your best, but don't base your self-identity and self-esteem on how things turn out. Determine to be satisfied and secure in God's unconditional acceptance of you. Ask God to use the situation to form you more into the image of Christ.

3. *Be genuine.*

Be careful not to present your ideal self to impress people. Try sharing a weakness or a personal struggle. (Or maybe you need to do the opposite and learn not to put yourself down as way of eliciting sympathy and instead share a personal strength or accomplishment.)

4. *Let people cut in front of you!*

When you're driving let people cut in front of you and pray for them as they do! Let go of your position or space on the road. Remind yourself that you're not just in your car, you're in God's kingdom with Christ and that's wonderful!

5. *Listen to others first.*

In a meeting let others speak first and promote their ideas. If you don't get to promote your agenda don't worry about it. God is enough for you!

6. *Don't be defensive.*

When someone misunderstands you or criticizes you don't defend yourself. Listen to their feelings, empathize, and entrust your reputation to God. If you know you're loved by God (and a safe friend outside of this test) you can *relax!*

As you take a situation like one of these and work on releasing control to God remember: *Don't just try, train!* We practice spiritual disciplines as means of grace, as ways to interact with God's generous favor so that we can start changing *on the inside.* Think of a spiritual exercise as a way to watch and pray with Jesus *before* you get into a stressful situation.

In prayer anticipate a scenario that tempts you to try hard to make things happen or to get frustrated and anxious. Imagine yourself in that situation and pray that the Lord God would help you to deny any pressing desires and submit fully to being in Jesus' yoke. Relax in this surrender and cultivate one desire: *to glorify God.* Watch to see what the Lord is doing. This is the easy-yoke-life of Christ. What peace it brings!

A Breath Prayer From the Bible

On the Cross Jesus let go of everything and abandoned all outcomes to his Abba. To help him do this he prayed Psalm 31:5: "Father, into your hands I commit my spirit" (Luke 23:46).

What situation do you need to bring into the yoke of the Sovereign Lord?

Let's spend a few minutes using this prayer of submission to watch and pray with Jesus in order to become the kind of person who in that situation will abandon outcomes to our Father who loves us.

As we did in Chapter One let's breathe our prayer, inhaling and exhaling the words of Jesus. Use your breathing to relax your body and mind in God's presence right now:

- Breathe in deep through your nose...

- Hold your breath...

- Exhale through your mouth...

- Breathe in: "Father..."

- Hold onto the word "Father" as you hold your breath...

- Breathe out: "Into your hands I commit my spirit."

You may want to meditate on Jesus' words as you imagine him on the cross, giving his life out of love for you and all people. He's in the most horrific, painful trial, but he's drawing strength from his Abba Father. He's turned loose of everything — his dignity, his reputation, his comfort, his body, his very life — and he expresses his total abandonment to God in his prayer: "Father... into your hands I commit my spirit."

Next, identify a situation in your life that is a challenge or a stress, something you're tempted to control. Then release this to the Sovereign Lord, praying, "Father... into your hands I commit _____."

Then throughout the day pause to breathe and shoot up our little arrow prayer,[33] "Father... into your hands I commit _____." Make a game of it and see how many times you can remind yourself to offer up this prayer! This will help you to submit yourself very practically to be *ruled* by the peace of Christ (Colossians 3:15).

Soul Talk

Recall from our Spiritual Formation Triangle that accepting our difficulties as learning opportunities is one of the most important things we can do for our spiritual growth.

1. What is one thing you learned about how you can live your daily life in Jesus' easy yoke?

2. What is a recent example in which you struggled with trying hard too hard to accomplish something, controlling a situation, or being anxious?

3. How did it go for you this week with abandoning an outcome to the Lord to get into his easy yoke? How did breathing Jesus' prayer of submission to the Father help you (or not)?

Three

Smiling in Your Storm (The Gospel)

In 2008 Kristi and I helped to lead a spiritual pilgrimage to Israel to "Walk Where Jesus Walked." A highlight for me was sailing the Sea of Galilee, the very same waters that Jesus sailed on and walked on! I recalled the story of the time that Jesus and his apostles were in their boat rowing when suddenly they got caught in a fierce storm.

That day when evening came, [Jesus] said to his disciples, "Let us go over to the other side." Leaving the crowd behind, they took him along, just as he was, in the boat. There were also other boats with him. A furious squall came up, and the waves broke over the boat, so that it was nearly swamped. Jesus was in the stern, sleeping on a cushion. The disciples woke him and said to him, "Teacher, don't you care if we drown?"

He got up, rebuked the wind and said to the waves, "Quiet! Be still!" Then the wind died down and it was *completely calm.*

He said to his disciples, "Why are you so afraid? Do you still have no faith?"

They were terrified and asked each other, "Who is this? Even the wind and the waves obey him!" (Mark 4:35-41).

"I Have to Fix This!"

Dark storm clouds pelted freezing rain on Jesus and the disciples, gale winds whipped their boat in circles, and wave after wave splashed into them and was swamping their boat. The disciples were rowing and rowing as hard and fast as they could to get out of the furious squall and make it safely to land, but they couldn't make any progress — they were stuck in the middle of the sea about to capsize and drown!

The disciples were soaked in panic. They were drenched in doom. *Yet Jesus was napping peacefully!* Finally, they screamed at him: "Help Jesus! We're going to drown! Don't you care about us?"

How would you react if you were caught at sea in a fierce storm? When you have a big problem how do you think about it? What belief system do you operate on when you're in trouble?

- "It's up to me to fix this — I can't count on anyone else."

- "If I don't solve this it'll be terrible."

- "Why won't he/she help me!"

- "I can't be happy until this problem is solved."

In a storm maybe you exhaust yourself, rowing as fast as you can to get out of it?

Being anxious about troubles becomes a life script for some. They stress and worry until their problem is solved. They complain. They may panic, have an emotional melt down, or get angry at someone. They have no peace or joy until their situation improves. And it's up to them (or someone) to fix things.

Life Events Stress Test

How is your stress level? What changes have you gone through in the last year that may be affecting your health and well-being? Health professionals have been using the highly researched "Life Events Stress Test" for over forty years. Countless people have taken it and found it very helpful.[34]

In the past 12 months, which of the following 42 major life events have taken place in your life? Place a check by each life event you've experienced and total the points at the bottom. Then check your vulnerability to stress-related illness.

____ 100 Death of Spouse

____ 73 Divorce

____ 65 Marital Separation or from relationship partner

____ 63 Jail Term

____ 63 Death of close family member

____ 53 Personal injury or illness

____ 50 Marriage

____ 47 Fired at work

____ 45 Marital reconciliation

____ 45 Retirement

____ 44 Change in family member's health

____ 40 Pregnancy

____ 39 Sex difficulties

____ 39 Addition to family

____ 39 Business readjustment

____ 38 Change in financial state

____ 37 Death of close friend

____ 36 Change to a different line of work

____ 35 Change in number of arguments with significant other

____ 31 Large mortgage or loan

____ 30 Foreclosure of mortgage or loan

____ 29 Change in work responsibilities

____ 29 Trouble with in-laws

____ 28 Outstanding personal achievement

____ 26 Spouse begins or stops work

____ 26 Starting or finishing school/college

____ 25 Change in living conditions

____ 24 Revision of personal habits

____ 23 Trouble with boss

____ 20 Change in work hours or conditions

____ 20 Change in residence

____ 20 Change in school/college

____ 19 Change in recreational habits

____ 19 Change in church activities

____ 18 Change in social activities

____ 17 Moderate mortgage or loan

____ 16 Change in sleeping habits

____ 15 Change in number of family gatherings

____ 15 Change in eating habits

____ 13 Vacation

____ 12 Christmas season

____ 11 Minor violations of the law

_____ *Total Life Stress Score*

Understanding Your Life Stress Score

Which stress level does your score fall in?

- 0-149: Low susceptibility to stress-related illness

- 150-299: Medium susceptibility to stress-related illness

- 300 and over: High susceptibility to stress-related illness

Notice that any change or responsibility, even a positive one, is a stress that adds pressure on you. People who experience high levels of stress are vulnerable to illness, especially if they *internalize stress as anxiety* or don't have the personal resources to cope. Stress related health problems range from mild problems like frequent tension headaches, acid indigestion, and loss of sleep to very serious illnesses like ulcers, hypertension, migraines, and cancer. Being over-stressed can also cause conflicts in relationship, anxiety disorders, depression, and burn out.

The question of this chapter is, *How are you and I responding to the stress storms that we get caught in?* Most of us react to pressure and problems by trying to fix our problem in our own strength. But is this a right way to think? Is it helpful?

High stress damages your body and soul — unless you react with confidence in God.

Celeste Laid Her Dream on God's Altar

Celeste was depressed. Since she was a little girl her dream was to be married and raise children, but here she was 42 years old and still single. "Why won't God give me the desire of my heart?" she complained to me. "Why doesn't he answer my prayers?"

It wasn't like she'd sat around at home waiting for God to help her. She'd dated men from her church singles group, a biking club, and Christian dating services. She'd read countless Christian books on relationships, prayer, and trusting God. She'd been in small groups and sought help in counseling. But what did she have to show for it? When she opened her closet there were bridesmaid dresses, but there was no wedding dress!

"I'm afraid to be an 'old maid' like my aunt," she cried. But just as quickly as the tears leaked out she put her finger in the dike, "I know I have to pick myself up and count my blessings."

Indeed, she had a busy social life with many good friends, she appreciated her church family, she went on mission trips, and she loved her job as the Human Resource Director for a Christian organization. These were good things, but "counting her blessings" to repress her grief was not good — *it was making her depressed.*

In therapy I helped Celeste to stop invalidating her sadness, verbalize it, and learn to receive empathy and comfort. We had to work on her self-esteem, helping her to stop punishing herself with self-hatred. Also, a major focus was her unresolved grief over losing her mother when she was six years old.

Six months later her depression was mostly improved, but she was still single and fighting it. She couldn't accept it. She *wouldn't* accept the possibility of being truly happy as a single woman.

One day, I took a risk and suggested something that was rather unorthodox for a therapist: *I invited her to make a sacrifice for God.* "The LORD asked Abraham to offer his son Isaac on the altar," I said. "Did he love God that much? Could he trust that even though it felt so wrong God would do something good?

"Abraham did. He gave his son to the LORD. He let go of his dream to be a father and put all his hope, not in getting what he wanted from the Lord, but simply in his relationship with him."

"I can't do that!" Celeste shot back at me. "I can't give up my dream — it's the longing of my heart to be married! That makes it seem like God doesn't love me at all!"

"I understand this feels wrong and bad," I replied softly. "Maybe I'm wrong for bringing it up, but you might read the story of Abraham in Genesis 22 and Hebrews 11 and pray about this."[35]

She left my office crying and I wasn't sure if she'd come back.

But a few weeks later she did return and she told me that after a lot of tears and anger and wrestling with God she finally decided to walk in the old way of Abraham. Then she had a breakthrough in the middle of the night when she had a dream about her relationship with Jesus. "I'm the bride of Jesus!" she exclaimed. "He's my First Love. Even if I never get married I can be happy if I know Jesus as my Friend and walk closely and sweetly with him."

I bet you know how the story ends! About four months after leaving her dream at the altar of the Lord, learning to accept her loss, and growing to delight more and more in Christ alone, she met a wonderful Christian man through a friend. They got married. She became a stepmother and a year later they adopted a seven-year old girl. And they served the Lord together through their church.

Don't Worry About Waves — See Jesus' Smile!

In my history I also have reacted to my problems by worrying, complaining, or getting frustrated. All I saw was the storm and so I worried about the waves that were threatening me. All I knew to do was to obsess on how I could row safely to shore. Perhaps I'd say a prayer, but generally I felt like I was on my own to fix my problems. My reality was the storm. My identity was tied up in how I dealt with wind and waves. My solution was to work hard and smart to make things better.

I didn't understand Jesus' nap in the tempest-tossed boat! How could he smile and sleep in a storm? How could he be so relaxed (there's that word for Jesus again!) when he was rain-soaked, chilled to the bone, the disciples were yelling, and everyone was in great peril? You might think he was calm because he was the Son of God and he knew he could calm the storm with a word. That's true, of course, but I don't think that's *why* he was calm.

Jesus was also a human being. The Bible tells us that he was tempted in every way that we are, including to worry and to give into fear (Hebrews 4:15-16). And he was tempted to take matters into his own hands and act on his own, without the Father (Matthew 4:1-11).

But Jesus wasn't just in the visible storm — *he had put himself in the invisible heavens.* He saw more than the waves — he saw many angels in action all around him. He heard more than thunder and wind whipping the boat — he heard the loving words of his Father. He didn't just feel cold and wet — he felt Holy

Spirit's presence. *Jesus was in the divine yoke, drawing on heavenly resources!*

So when Jesus awoke to face the storm he simply spoke the word of his Father, as he always did (John 14:10, 24). He spoke the peace of God from his body into wind, waves, and disciples.

Jesus napping peacefully in the storm-tossed boat is the hidden miracle in this story.

It's like in Matthew 11. The storm there was the religious towns of Galilee rejecting his ministry to their own destruction. In the midst of this distress, Matthew reports, "Abruptly, Jesus broke into prayer: 'Thank you, Father, Lord of heaven and earth...'" He's in the grace-yoke of the Father and he speaks "tenderly," inviting us to experience the "Father and Son intimacies."

Throughout his life Jesus faced all kinds of trials, injustices, and hardships and he didn't anxiously rush to fix them on his own — he relied on his Father with him and followed his lead.[36]

I Smiled in My Storm

Even as I was writing the first edition of this book a storm tested me. Looking back it was just a little thundercloud, but I felt attacked. A Christian leader condemned me as a "heretic" for teaching that people could actually become more like the Son of God and for using "contemplative spirituality." On his website he posted a picture of my wife and me with disparaging remarks about us. Clearly, he'd be upset if when he got to heaven he found out I was his roommate! Especially if I invited him to "meditate" on a Psalm!

For this man to disagree with our doctrine was fine — on some points he might be right and I might be wrong — but the contempt for Kristi and me that he spewed out to the world was hurtful! In my nature I am eager to do good and to please other people and I am sensitive to criticism. So in years past my normal reaction to being harshly judged, especially in public by a Christian leader, was to scurry to fix my reputation so I didn't have to be embarrassed (which is the deceitful and stress-inducing, "I have to fix this myself!" mentality). Or I might get angry. But in this case I did neither.

That day I had prayed The Apprentice Prayer with these lines:

Dear Father, I ask you to ordain the events of this day and use them to make me more like Jesus. I trust you Sovereign Lord, that you won't let anything happen to my family or me today, except that it passes through your loving hands. So no matter what problems, hardships, or injustices I face today help me not to worry or get frustrated, but instead to relax in the yoke of your providence. Yes, today I will rejoice because I am in your eternal kingdom, you love me, and you are teaching me...

"Blessed are those who are persecuted... for theirs is the kingdom of heaven." (Matthew 5:10)

So I thanked God that I was being persecuted for Christ — and that this Christian leader had devoted himself to teaching others Biblical doctrine as best he could. I prayed for God's blessing on this man and his ministry, that God would draw him closer to Christ, encourage him in his study of Christian doctrine, and use him to bring more and more people into God's truth for life.

I believe that Christ came out of my heart naturally in this trial (I wish this was always the case!) because for some years now Christ has been teaching me to do all that I do in God's Government of Grace. This includes regularly praying Psalms of

Lament and other Scriptures in which I practice relaxing in Abba's arms in anticipation of coming storms and then when the storms hit I'm already rejoicing in God's kingdom rule and less prone to react with stress or agitation.

Jesus' Easy Yoke Gospel sets us free to smile in our storms. Sadly, few people today understand, much less live in terms of, this Gospel that Jesus preached.

The Gospels We Commonly Hear Today

For many years Dallas Willard has asked people, "Why is it that so many Christians today don't look much like Christ?" He says it is because *they believe a different gospel than the one Jesus preached.*[37] Here are three common versions of the gospel:

1. *The Conservative Gospel on the Right.*

   "Believe the right facts about Jesus and you'll be forgiven of your sin and let into heaven when you die."

   Jesus died to pay for our sins and rose from the dead if we will only believe this then we will be forgiven of our sins and go to heaven when we die. Getting our doctrinal facts right (e.g., by studying the Bible) removes our guilt and gets us into heaven when we die.

2. *The Social Gospel on the Left.*

   "Love other people, especially the poor and needy, and God will accept you and let you into heaven when you die."

   Jesus came and gave his life to love the oppressed, liberating them to be all that they can be. Ministries of compassion and healing, social justice causes, support groups, counseling, and other ways of helping hurting people as Jesus did is *the* purpose of life and how we get into heaven.

3. *Consumer Christianity.*

   "Ask God and he'll bless you like you want. He'll help make your project of a successful life turn out. Go to church to get your needs met and feel better. Take care of your church and it will take care of you."

We use God's grace for the forgiveness we need and the blessings we want. The church is our spiritual shopping mall in which we "buy" whatever services we need to take care of ourselves or to get God to take care of us. We expect the services of the church to entertain us and to meet our "felt needs" and in turn the church expects us to give money and use our gifts to serve.

I was raised on the Conservative Gospel. Then training to be a psychologist I gravitated toward a hybrid of the second and third ones. How about you? Which gospel do you most relate to?

Each of these three gospels is somewhat true. Faith in Christ, his cross and resurrection are essential. Christians are called to love others, including the poor and needy. God does want to bless us and our participation in a local church. But the partial gospels miss the mark. In each case it's easy for me to "believe and do" the message, *but still remain in charge of my daily life activities*. As long as I have the right doctrine, do good works, or take care of my church I'm thought to be "in."

What's missing? *The opportunity to become an apprentice to the crucified and risen Christ in the Kingdom of Love.*

To be in the Kingdom of God submit to Christ's leadership and rely on his Spirit.

Jesus' Gospel of the Kingdom of God

What is the Kingdom of God? Dallas Willard answers that a "kingdom" simply is the effective range of someone's will. You and I have a kingdom or queendom — things, activities, and even people that we're in charge of. For instance, if someone starts rummaging through your purse or wallet you feel violated, "Hey, that's mine! What are you doing?" That's part of your kingdom that you've been given responsibility for.

God's kingdom is simply God in action; it's where what God wants done is done, which is why Jesus taught us to pray to the Father, "Thy kingdom come, Thy will be done on earth as it is in heaven" (Matthew 6:10).

But we may think of the Kingdom of God as being far off and way later. We've been taught that the people of the first century rejected Jesus' kingdom and so now we all have to wait until we go to heaven or when Jesus returns to earth to enter his Eternal Dominion. So in this life we're left to "hang on" in our struggle with sin and keep seeking forgiveness while we wait for future peace and glory. It's like we've had car trouble and pulled off to the side of the highway while we wait for the Heavenly AAA to come and take us home to heaven!

Our Redeemer's Good News is that you have the opportunity now to become his apprentice in kingdom-living. He says, "Repent for the Kingdom of the Heavens is at hand" (Matthew 4:17).[38]

The idea here is to *think again* about our strategy for life in the light of this wonderful new opportunity that God's kingdom is open. *You are loved by the King of kings!* Hold onto life on your terms and you're living an empty, loveless, dead life, but lose your life for Christ and you'll discover abundant, eternal life. Run your life as you see fit and you'll get nowhere, but submit to Jesus — ask him to govern your thoughts, desires, and all that you say and do — and you'll learn how to live your ordinary life in the reality of the heavenly realms with him, now and forever.

If heaven starts to get into you now then getting into heaven when you die will take care of itself! The Savior, the Holy One, who sacrificed himself for us, offers us God's kind of life — real and abundant life — that begins just as soon as we offer our lives to him, submitting to his eternal rule.

Don't wait until you die to go to heaven —
start living in the heavens with Christ today!

What Good News this is! We don't have to fix our own problems or just hang on in our difficult life till we die and go to heaven, but we can actually grow in the blessings of God's grace and righteousness now as we submit to Jesus Christ and rely on him. (It is important to say that Jesus' kingdom being available to us now does not deny that in eternity there will be for us a glorious new manifestation of the kingdom!)

Our opportunity is to let our kingdom or queendom be taken over by God's rule, to submit our will to the will of our Father, to do all that we do with the Lord and according to his leadership. In this way we enjoy the benefits of being kingdom dwellers and we're prepared to minister his compassionate rule to others.

The Gospel of the Kingdom is *the* Gospel

Again and again — over 100 times in the Gospels! — Jesus invited people to participate with him in the Kingdom of God. He communicated this through parables, healing, and teaching. Of course, he varies his wording, but his theme does not change.

When Christ was resurrected and appeared to his disciples over 40 days he continued to talk to them about life in the Kingdom of God (Acts 1:3). He did not change his message to say, "Since all the people have rejected me as their king everyone will have to wait to enter my kingdom until my second coming or until they die and go to heaven."

Jesus trained his apprentices to preach and manifest his Gospel of the Kingdom: "As you go, proclaim the good news, 'The kingdom of heaven has come near.' Cure the sick, raise the dead, cleanse the lepers, cast out demons" (Matthew 10:5-8).

Some theologians say that the Apostle Paul did not preach a kingdom Gospel, but *the Gospel of Christ and his cross is the Gospel of the Kingdom!* To say that Christ is Lord or Master is a Gentile way of saying he is King. (The Gentiles had an emperor and the Jews had a king.)

Acts records Paul talking to people "persuasively about the kingdom of God" (Acts 19:8) and "welcoming all who came to him, proclaiming the kingdom of God and teaching about the Lord Jesus Christ with all boldness and without hindrance" (Acts 28:30-31). Fourteen times in his epistles Paul teaches explicitly on the Kingdom of God. For instance he prays: "For [God] has rescued us from the dominion of darkness and brought us into the kingdom of the Son he loves, in whom we have redemption, the forgiveness of sins" (Colossians 1:13-14).

The cross of Christ is the gate to the Kingdom of the Heavens.

The Gospel of the Kingdom is Countercultural

Jesus spoke bold words that were offensive to many people when he said: "I am the way and the truth and the life. No one comes to the Father except through me" (John 14:6). But I'm afraid that you and I who know the truth of God and call ourselves "Christ-followers" may, nonetheless, be prone to miss *the way* of Christ by being swept up into the way of our culture without realizing it. To know the truth of Jesus isn't enough to have his divine life flowing through us — *we also need to know the way or attitude of Jesus.* (Recall that in Acts the first Christians were called followers of "the Way."[39])

When we have a problem in our family, organization, or church who is our first and primary consultant? Who do we rely on for help and to give us advice? Probably an expert or a professional. That's fine, but *are we looking to the Lord God in our midst?* That's what Jesus always did and when we look to our Savior he brings us the fullness of God!

In our time of need we may not have the thought that *Jesus is the smartest person alive and he is available to consult with!*[40]

Jesus is the smartest person and best consultant for any need!

Our Lord and Savior is our Wonderful Counselor and in him are hid all treasures of wisdom and knowledge (Isaiah 9:6, Colossians 2:3). As I do what I'm doing *I can step into the King's classroom and learn from him how he would do what I'm doing if he were me.* When I look to people for help I see them as Christ's ambassadors to me, even if they don't identify with that. I relinquish my expectations for particular blessings and pray as in The Apprentice Prayer, *"I want to be all and only for you Jesus!"*

Discovering that Jesus truly was her portion — even if she was an "old maid" without a child — is what set Celeste free. The culture told her that she needed to make her marriage dream come true to be happy, but the Bible told her that if she laid her dream down at the Altar of the Lord and followed Jesus she'd have the best life in God's kingdom! The Triangle of Soul Transformation helps us understand how we can respond to God's grace as Celeste did:

• Believe Jesus' Gospel and delight in the Lord.

• Accept life storms as tests of character and opportunities to learn to identify with Christ Jesus.

• Practice disciplines like giving thanks to God.[41]

Giving Thanks in Trials (Beatitudes)

Our Prince of Peace told us to expect troubles and to "take heart" from him and how he dealt with them (Matthew 9:22; Mark 6:50; John 16:33). The Apostles in their many persecutions and sufferings encouraged us to follow the Lord's example:

- Paul taught, "Give thanks in all circumstances for this is God's will for you in Christ Jesus" (1 Thessalonians 5:18).

- James, the brother of our Lord, agreed, "Consider it pure joy... whenever you face trials of many kinds" (James 1:2).

- Peter also urged us to praise God in difficult and painful situations (1 Peter 1:3-9).

Being thankful when we have problems? Having "pure joy" in pain and injustice? Praising God when things go wrong?

William Law (1686-1761), an evangelical devotional writer of three centuries ago from the Anglican tradition, understood giving thanks to God in trials. The Englishman gave up a promising career as a priest in the university or the church when he refused to swear allegiance to the new monarch. He settled for working as a tutor and a writer. He accepted his unfortunate lot with a positive attitude and urged others to follow his example:

There is no state of mind so holy, so excellent, and so truly perfect as that of thankfulness to God. Consequently, nothing is of more importance in religion than that which exercises and improves this habit of mind. The greatest saint in the world is he who is always thankful to God, who wills everything God wills, who receives everything as an instance of God's goodness, and who has a heart always ready to praise God...

If anyone would tell you the shortest, surest way to all happiness and all perfection, he must tell you to make a rule to yourself to thank and praise God for everything that happens to you... This thankful spirit... heals and turns all that it touches into happiness.

For this reason I exhort you to this method in your devotion that every day may be made a day of thanksgiving, and that the spirit of murmur and discontent may be unable to enter into the heart that is so often employed in singing the praises of God.[42]

Gratitude to God is the source of virtue and joy.

In The Apprentice Prayer after accepting our tribulations we exclaim with gratitude to God, "Yes, today I will rejoice because I am in your eternal kingdom, you love me, and you are teaching me!" Even in bad circumstances the Kingdom of the Heavens is present for us and it's flowing with rivers of righteousness, peace, and joy (Romans 14:17). *Let's drink in!*

We're shifting our focus from the storm thundering to the Lord resting. Instead of stressing out over changing our unhappy situation, we're praying to change our unhappy *self*, focusing on the one thing in life that we're responsible for, which also is our greatest opportunity: *asking Jesus to teach us how to become more like him.*

Paul helps us adjust our perspective. He says that our troubles are "light and momentary" and the image of Christ that God is forming in us is "an eternal glory that outweighs them all." When we "fix our eyes on" this we are "renewed day by day" (2 Corinthians 4:16-18). Accordingly, I like to pray along these lines:

Lord Jesus, you are wonderful to me and you are doing something good that I'm not yet seeing. So I'm watching to see what you're doing in this situation and what you want to teach me. I'm ready to join with you in the work of your kingdom and to follow you however you lead me in this trial.

Peter elaborated on why we can thank God in the middle of our trials, saying that by God's mercy through Christ we have been given "new birth into a living hope" — the hope of enjoying the glory of heaven with the Lord forever *and* the "inexpressible and glorious joy" that right now we are receiving the salvation of souls (1 Peter 1:3-9).

In other words, what brings us joy in our trials is that *we are alive eternally in the great land in which the rising Son comes to us from heaven!* (Luke 1:78). Christ the King rose from the dead and he is with us, loving us and shaping us in his image, refining our faith like gold in the fire (1 Peter 1:7). Our Lord is developing us to grow in our intimacy with him and our capacity to partner with him in his work.

We may suffer great losses, injustices, or pain and from the world's perspective things may not go well for us. But if we realize that we can thrive in The Kingdom — and therefore do not need to be overwhelmed by or defined by our problem situation — then we have reason to be *wonderfully happy!*

The way to be happy in God during our trials is to *practice it,* cultivating a joyful-faith-in-Christ-mindset to bring into our problems. Jesus' beatitudes help us to do this.

Meditate on Jesus' Beatitudes

"Blessed are the poor in spirit," our eternal Bridegroom proclaims. "For theirs is the Kingdom of the Heavens. Blessed are those who mourn, for they will be comforted" (Matthew 5:3-4).

Prior to her Abraham journey, Celeste's attitude was like the typical way we read the beatitudes: *"If* I'm poor in spirit then God will accept me in his kingdom. *If* I mourn over my sins and losses then he'll comfort me." These are generally true, but, as Dallas Willard illuminates in *The Divine Conspiracy,* this is *not* what Jesus means.[43] *He's not telling us to do anything.* He's simply saying, "Those who are spiritually bankrupt or grieving a loss are divinely blessed when they realize that the Kingdom of the Heavens is open to them."

In Jesus' day everyone thought you had to be like the Pharisees to be blessed by God, but he's saying, "Those who are up in the world are actually down if they're not in God's kingdom and those who are down in the world are actually up if they're in God's kingdom."[44]

The heavenly happiness that Jesus proclaims in the beatitudes is not in meeting a condition — it's in belonging to the Kingdom. *Maybe we put the blessing in the condition so we can engineer our way into a happier life?*

The blessings of Jesus' beatitudes are not in their conditions, but in the *Kingdom.*

But the divine Rabbi has something much better for us than "Principles for Healthy Living" or "How to Get Your Blessing." He's saying, "Give up your project of trying to make your life turn out the way you want it to. Forget about performing to get God's favor. Look, I'm here to forgive your shortcomings and open the way for you to live in the Father's world with me. Follow me and you'll experience real life!"

For instance, Jesus says, "Blessed are the peacemakers, for they will be called children of God" (Matthew 5:9). His point is not, "It's a blessing to get in the middle of an argument" — *just ask a police officer about that!* Christ is telling people who are caught in conflict that *even there* they can experience the joy of belonging in God's family. (Of course, it's a good thing to seek to bring peace to people in conflict, but this is not what Jesus is teaching here.)

If we understood our Bible then we wouldn't be shocked to read the beatitudes this way. Similar divine promises of favor on the unlikely and unfortunate are in the song of Moses and Miriam (Exodus 15), Hannah's prayer (1 Samuel 2:1-11), the Psalms (34, 37, 107:31-43, 113), Ezekiel's prophecy (17:22-24), Mary's magnificat (Luke 1:46-55), and Zechariah's song (Luke 1:68-79).[45]

The Key to Heavenly Treasure!

Why is it so important *how* we read the beatitudes? Because at the beginning of his masterpiece sermon the Lord is handing us the key to the *treasure store of God's glorious kingdom.* He's offering us the best wisdom for life that's ever been shared, but to be able to make use of it we need to be submitted to the Lord and living from his reign of goodness and grace.

Jesus begins his discourse on the hill (also the one on the plain) by bringing the happy news that God's royal realm is available to *anyone* who will come to him. Just look at the apostles he chose — no one would've chosen them! They're examples of the poor in the spirit. They had no religious education and no money. They didn't have a chance of getting into a rabbi's school. A tax collector. An uncircumcised Greek. Men that smell like fish. People thinking about violent revolution.

The Son of God was kind and generous to societal rejects of all kinds. He forgave prostitutes and all "sinners." He touched lepers. He healed the sick and delivered demoniacs. He ate with tax collectors. He befriended despised foreigners. He loved the "down and out." This got him in big trouble with the elitist religious leaders!

The beatitudes also challenge Western culture *today*. We think the good life is reserved for the good looking and popular. So Dallas offers some silly paraphrases that convey Jesus' true spirit:

Blessed are those who smell bad...
The too big, too little, too loud,
The bald, the fat, and the old —
For they are all riotously celebrated in the party of Jesus![46]

"The last will be first, and the first will be last" (Matthew 20:16).

But to be sure, Christ also welcomes the "up and in" to be part of God's Glorious Universe. Pharisees like Nicodemus and Joseph of Arimathea joined his ranks, as did Roman centurions, and Joanna, the wife of Herod's manager. They were welcomed in the group as long as they accepted the likes of Mary Magdalene, who Jesus delivered of seven demons.

Jesus says to this diverse crowd that follows him:

Blessed are you who are uneducated in the spiritual life for you can live in the Kingdom of the Heavens.

Blessed are you who are grieving a loss for you can experience God's comfort.

Blessed are you who are shy for you can inherit the best the earth has to offer.

Blessed are you who have been wrongly treated and long for justice for you can be filled with God's life.

Blessed are you who are tender-hearted toward the wounded and needy for you can know God's tender-heart for you.

Blessed are you who pursue seemingly unattainable ideals for you can find God.

Blessed are you who are caught in the middle of conflict for you can be at peace as God's child.

Blessed are you who are persecuted badly for you can live in the Kingdom of the Heavens where there is reason to jump for joy! (Matt. 5:3-12, paraphrased).

Write Your Own "Blesseds"

To experience God's favor Celeste had to re-think her world view. How could it be a blessing to be an "old maid"? It's a stretch. But she came to trust that even as an older single woman *there was real happiness with Jesus as the Bridegroom of her heart.*

There are many other circumstances that also may seem unblessable to us. Cancer. Bankruptcy. Getting a DUI. Becoming divorced. Pastoring a small or shrinking church.[47] Finishing your life alone in a nursing home.

God doesn't *cause* us to suffer in these ways. Generally, he doesn't even want painful trials for us, but, for good reasons he allows them. So we need to accept our trials and feel the strain of bringing them into *the larger spiritual reality* of the sovereign Trinity's universe. There we'll discover how blessed we are — even when our physical situation isn't improved.

Personalizing Jesus' beatitudes had a *huge* impact on me. My stress didn't go away, but increasingly my anxiety did. It surprised me that this relief came not from seeking it, but from *seeking Christ and his kingdom with greater intelligence and passion.* Here were some of the "kingdom proclamations"[48] that I heard at the beginning of my renewal:

- "Blessed are you Bill with financial insecurity for yours is the Kingdom of the Heavens."

- "Blessed are you Bill with family tensions for you can be at peace as a child of God."

- "Blessed are you Bill with Celiac's Disease for every spiritual blessing is yours in Christ."

- "Blessed are you Bill when you are criticized for your Father in the heavens is smiling over you."

- "Blessed are you Bill that God has asked you to give up your dream of writing books for the Author of Life is writing your story." (I used this idea to help Celeste get unstuck.)

What problems are you struggling with? What is diminishing your happiness today? Receive Jesus' "Great Reversal" by writing (and speaking out loud): "Blessed are you (your name) with (your problem) for yours is the Kingdom of the Heavens."

"Blessed are the sat upon, spat upon, ratted on" (Simon and Garfunkle).[49]

A Breath Prayer From the Bible

Our Breath Prayer from Scripture this week is the words of Jesus in the storm: "Peace. Be still."

In the spirit of Jesus' kingdom beatitudes we want to meditate on his words of peace to shift our focus from struggling to get out of our personal storm to *learning to rest with Jesus in Abba Father's arms while in the trial.* Breathing in and out the blessed peace of Christ can help us to settle into it till it takes over our life..

Take a few minutes while lying in bed, in a quiet chair, while you're driving or waiting for someone, or as you take a walk to meditate on Jesus' words: "Peace. Be Still" (Mark 4:39).

To help you contemplate imagine Jesus sleeping in the boat and resting in Abba's arms as the storm rages on and on. *See the calm sea in Jesus' soul* in the midst of all the storm's turmoil and danger and pray, "Peace. Be still."

It's helpful to breathe Jesus' words in and out. Breathe in slow and deep: "Peace..." Hold your breath... Exhale: "Be still..."

In prayer fill your *spiritual* lungs with the Word and the Spirit... Hold them in your heart... Release and relax... Repeat this prayer till you sense the reality of God's peace in your body.

Then talk to the Lord of the Seas about one of your stormy trials. Imagine yourself in this situation while you contemplate Jesus' words: "Peace... Be still..."

Ask God to help you bring his comfort to someone today by praying for them: "Peace... Be still..."

How many times could you remember to pray Jesus' words this week? Make learning to practice God's presence fun!

Soul Talk

Immanuel said, "You're here to be salt-seasoning that brings out the God-flavors of this earth. If you lose your saltiness, how will people taste godliness?" (Matthew 5:13, MSG). Sharing your *Easy Yoke* journey with friends brings out the God-flavor in your lives. Being salty also helps you preserve what God is teaching you *and* makes you thirsty for more of God!

1. What is one thing you learned about Jesus' kingdom gospel?

2. What is a problem that you're struggling with? What personal beatitude does the Lord have for you in your trial?

3. What effect did praying "Peace... Be still" have on your ability to rejoice in the midst of a trial this week?

Four

Jumping Into Abba's Arms!

Some years ago I had a delightful experience that I'll never forget. I was about to drive home from my office and I called home first. Our youngest daughter, Briana, who was seven years old at the time, answered and I told her that I would be home in five minutes and that I had a hug to give her.

When I walked in the door she was right there waiting for me, perched atop the banister end cap. She jumped down and ran toward me shouting, "433 seconds! 433 seconds!"

"What do you mean?" I asked with bewilderment.

"It took you 433 seconds to get home Daddy!" And she leaped up into my arms…

Just telling the story melts my heart all over again, even many years later. How blessed I am to have a daughter who loves me like that!

With all three of my children when they were little and heard me coming home from work they'd yell from our family room in the back of the house, "Daddy's home!" They'd say, "Daddy, wait there at the door." And then one-by-one they'd sprint the full length of the house and jump into my arms for a hug!

Sometimes this ritual was followed by what we came to call "Rough and Tough," which was a game of chasing the kids around the house to catch them in order to wrestle, tickle, and throw them onto a couch.

These are very special memories in part because my dad did the same thing with me. The "Daddy's home!" moment was often the highlight of my day as a little boy too.

Now I want to ask you (and myself!) a question…

Would you count the seconds before you could jump into the arms of your Heavenly Father? Is being Jesus' disciple the *delight* of your heart? Can you imagine becoming a person like that?

When was the last time you felt excited to connect with your Heavenly Father?

Jessica Didn't Trust God

"I can't *really* trust God," Jessica admitted to me. She couldn't imagine jumping with joy into the arms of God. She was a Christian and in her doctrine she believed in Christ and in the goodness of God, but in her heart she didn't feel safe depending on him.

"Where was God when my father sexually abused me?" she cried. "How could God allow seven years of letting my body be used for my father's perversion? I was just a little girl. I didn't even know what sex was. He damaged me beyond repair.

"It's so confusing to me. The same dad who made me laugh and bought me nice things violated me! And he made me feel physical pleasure about something so gross! Then to add to the shame of it all, later I acted this out by getting into sexual relationships, not only with boyfriends, but even with a married man. I'm so mad about this! My life has been ruined!"

Many nights Jessica cried out to God that the dark shadow wouldn't come into her room again, but it kept coming back. And when it did she froze in mute fear. She endured the pain by *dissociating,* pretending she wasn't there and shutting down her emotions.

Her father threatened her that if she ever told anyone about their "special secret" that she'd be sent away from the family. A few times she took the risk of trying to tell her mother, but she didn't believe her. This "special secret" was really a dirty secret. Who could she tell? Her pet cat — *really*. Jessica's cat listened to her cry and purred in her lap. No one else knew.

Jessica's image of God was that he had a mean side like her father. And yet at times she also saw God as passive like her mom because he allowed her to be violated.

I've talked with many people whose image of God was damaged as child by a parent, teacher, pastor, or coach because of abuse: sexual, physical, or emotional. When the abusive adult was a Christian the injury and confusion are even worse.

"I Can't *Really* Trust Anyone"

If you were Jessica could you trust God? Imagine yourself in her position. To one degree or another, we've all trusted and been wounded or disappointed in life. It may have been through your parents divorcing, a care-giver dying, a family conflict, a loved one's addiction, a spouse cheating on you, people at church mistreating you, or a friend disappearing in a time of need.

We may try to minimize our pain and problems by comparing ourselves to people like Jessica who have had a harder life. But this is *not* helpful. We need to be honest before God and one another about any hurts or injustices that have shaped our own ability to trust.

We might say that we "know" God is loving, but in our hearts, in our life experience, do we *truly know* God as good and kind? (Biblically, to know God is not head knowledge, it's to be in an interactive, intimate relationship with him.) We say that we trust God, but deep down inside do we trust him enough to submit ourselves *completely* to him? Maybe we feel that in some ways we need to hold back on being vulnerable with others and just rely on ourselves.

Real knowledge of God is spelled:
"i-n-t-i-m-a-c-y w-i-t-h J-e-s-u-s."

When I listen to the hearts of wounded people I often hear these narratives:

- "Be strong. Don't cry."

- "Children are to be seen, not heard."

- "Grin and bear it till the pain goes away."

- "Don't be needy — you'll burden people."

- "You have to watch your back!"

- "Pull yourself up by the bootstraps!"

These are unhealthy *and unholy* attitudes. Believing that you can't trust anyone shrinks your heart. To whatever extent you hold back from being vulnerable with the safe people who are accessible to you then you are missing out on the love you need and you'll be diminished in your capacity to love others fully.

You might think that you can trust God without trusting safe people, but it doesn't work that way. Jesus makes this point in his Greatest Commandment that links loving the God who loves us and loving our neighbor as ourselves (Mark 12:29-30). The Apostle John in his first letter teaches about the inseparable connection between how we relate with God and how we relate to other people (1 John 3:17-18, 4:11-12).

We learn to trust the God we can't see by trusting people that we can see. When we've been emotionally wounded by people we experience repair by finding someone that we can trust and sharing our heart and learning to do this as unto Christ. This is why in the Bible Christians are called "the body of Christ" (1

Corinthians 12:27) or "Christ's Ambassadors" (2 Corinthians 5:20).

When you have heart wounds that haven't healed or developmental needs that haven't been met it profoundly affects how you view and trust God, yourself, and other people.

Your emotional wounds affect your image of God and how you experience him.

What is Your Image of God?

Many years ago I developed the God Image Questionnaire (GIQ) to help people better understand how they see and experience God on a personal level.[50] To assess your inner, heart-felt image of God each question asks about your *personal experience* of God in daily life. Your experience of God is your attitudes, emotions, and interaction with God in response to your observations of what God seems to be doing or not doing in your life.

Do not answer the questions according to your opinions or theological beliefs about God. In other words, don't just give the "right" answers! Respond according to your *personal experience of God* or how you actually tend to relate to God.

Read each question and then circle "T" for mostly true or "F" for mostly false:

1. At times I don't trust that God is giving His full attention to the details of my life. T F

2. When I need God sometimes I observe that He does not help me very much. T F

3. In my experience God may withhold good things from me. T F

4. Sometimes I experience being disregarded by God.   T   F

5. If I feel that God is distant from me I tend to act on my own.
T   F

6. At times I give into pressure from God to do something that I don't want to do. T   F

7. Sometimes I do something to obtain God's favor. T   F

8. Sometimes I try to measure up to God's expectations so He won't be displeased with me. T   F

9. Even after I confess my sins to God I don't always trust that I'm forgiven. T   F

10. At times I'm not confident that God is treating me fairly. T   F

11. If I'm in a threatening situation I tend not to trust that God will protect me. T   F

12. At times I'm not sure that what I can do for God is important to Him. T   F

13. Sometimes I am unsure about whether or not God has a good purpose for my future. T   F

14. When I really need God I tend to feel left on my own. T   F

15. When I talk to God about a decision I need to make sometimes it seems he's not very interested. T   F

16. Sometimes I don't trust that God is really helping me with my problems. T   F

17. At times I don't trust that God wants to give me good things.
T   F

18. At times it's hard for me to truly believe that I am esteemed highly by God. T   F

19. Sometimes I don't trust that God is really with me to care for me. T   F

20. In my experience sometimes God doesn't give me freedom to do what I want. T   F

21. When I want God to do something for me I feel I should do something for Him to help my cause. T   F

22. At times I don't trust that God really approves of me. T   F

23. In my experience after I tell God I am sorry for my wrongdoing it feels like He may still be upset with me. T   F

24. Sometimes I avoid being honest with God because I don't want to be under judgment. T   F

25. If someone takes advantage of me then I tend to get upset that God didn't protect me. T   F

26. Sometimes I'm unsure if God believes in my abilities. T   F

27. At times I am not confident that God has special plans for me. T   F

28. In difficult situations I may not trust God to be at my side. T   F

To score your GIQ follow these steps:

1. Count one point for each "false" answer.

2. Add up the total for each row (aspect of God's perfect love). Scores should range from 0 to 2. Scores of 2 indicate your God Image strengths; these are areas where you have a positive experience of that aspect of God's love. Scores of 0 indicate your God Image weaknesses; you're struggling to feel God's love and need help in these dimensions.

3. Add up your total GIQ score for all 14 rows combined. Scores should range from 0 to 28. Higher scores mean a closer and more loving relationship with God, an image of God that is more positive and true to the God of the Bible.

Understanding Your GIQ

The "GIQ Table" below has 14 rows, one for each of the 14 aspects of God's perfect love — two times seven is a double emphasis on perfection! — from 1 Corinthians 13:4-7. ("Love never fails" in verse 8 is understood as a summary of all the characteristics of divine love.)

The first term for each aspect of love in the table is from the Bible's Love Chapter. There are two questions ("Quest") for each aspect. "False" answers to any question on the GIQ indicate a generally and usually positive experience of God's love (or image of God) in that particular aspect. "True" answers admit to struggling in that area of experiencing God's unfailing love.

GIQ Table		
Questions	**Aspect of God's Love**	**Score**
1, 15	Patient: attentive, interested	
2, 16	Kind: helpful	
3, 17	Not envious: generous, gives good gifts	
4, 18	Not boastful: esteems others highly	
5. 19	Not proud: close, available	
6, 20	Not rude: gives freedom, gentle	
7, 21	Not self-seeking: unconditional favor	
8, 22	Not easily angered: considerate	
9, 23	No record of wrongs: forgiving, merciful	
10, 24	Rejoices in truth, not evil: fair	
11, 25	Protects: keeps safe, defends	
12, 26	Trusts: respects, believes the best	
13, 27	Hopeful: has good plans	
14, 28	Perseveres: reliable, faithful	

Oh, to See God as He Is!

We all tend to project onto God from our life experience. Our heart's view of God is readily shaped by the way that our parents and other caregivers related to us early in life. As little people we internalize the messages that are spoken or implicit and then these color the lenses we use to view others, particularly God. For instance, a man who is emotionally detached says, "God is distant from me." Or a woman who struggles with anger, including at herself, experiences God as harsh and punitive.

To trust God's love we need to begin to experience it in our human relationships.

A.W. Tozer (1897-1963), one of the greatest pastors and writers of the 20th Century, said,

> What comes into our minds when we think about God is the most important thing about us...

> That our idea of God corresponds as nearly as possible to the true being of God is of immense importance to us. Compared with our actual thoughts about Him, our creedal statements are of little consequence. Our real idea of God may lie buried under the rubbish of conventional religious notions and may require an intelligent and vigorous search before it is finally unearthed and exposed for what it is. Only after an ordeal of painful self-probing are we likely to discover what we actually believe about God.

> A right conception of God is basic not only to systematic theology but to practical Christian living as well...

> The man [or woman] who comes to a right belief about God is relieved of ten thousand temporal problems.[51]

In 1 Corinthians 13 Paul says we see God's perfect love "through a glass darkly" and only "know in part." And in his letters he emphasizes that we need to be as Christ to one another by incarnating God's grace. This is a primary way that Christ heals our hurts and clears up our image of God so that we can grow to trust God from our hearts and appreciate his love.

Why Does God Allow Unjust Suffering?

Do you trust that God has always been good to you? Are you confident that his love for you is unfailing? Here's a litmus test: Look back over your personal history and consider times you were mistreated or experienced hardship... Can you see God caring for you despite your circumstances to the contrary? Can you say honestly and gratefully, "The Lord has been good to me!"?

Or try this test: How do you react when you see or hear about a child starving in Africa or a drunk driver killing a teenager? Do you trust that God genuinely and immediately cares for the one in peril? The one who died? The loved ones who are grieving?

This issue causes problems for many of us. Why does a good and powerful God allow innocent people to suffer?

The Bible wrestles with the question of innocent people suffering, especially in the Psalms. In all instances God doesn't answer our why question directly, not even when Jesus borrows the words of David from Psalm 22:1 and cries out, while being tortured to death on the cross: "My God, my God why have you forsaken me?"

Jesus on the cross *is* God's response to the pain and injustice that we suffer from. His shed blood is our source of comfort, forgiveness, and daily sustenance. His life sacrificed is our opportunity for divine living in the spiritual Promise Land.

On the cross Jesus knew the *immediate spiritual reality* of God's loving presence and purposes. Paul learned to respond to hard times the same way:

> Therefore we do not lose heart. Though outwardly we are wasting away, yet inwardly we are being renewed day by day. For our light and momentary troubles are achieving for us an eternal glory that far outweighs them all. So we fix our eyes not on what is seen, but on what is unseen. For what is seen is temporary, but what is unseen is eternal (2 Corinthians 4:16-18).

God's answer to our suffering
is Christ on the cross.

Right now Christ, our crucified and risen Lord and Savior, our eternal King, is actually in our midst with his angels! We may not connect with him, we may not even have a thought about him, but, nonetheless, always he is literally present in Spirit and is ready to care for us and help us — *if only we will reach out for his hand of grace.* And if we didn't know how to do that in the past then with the Lord who was, is, and is to come we can go back into our memory and invite him to show himself and minister his love. (In Chapter Ten we'll do this.)

Jesus didn't leave us as orphans, but gave us his Spirit — the Strengthener, the gift of the Father — to be with us always (John 14:16-18, Acts 1:4). He told us that each child (and by extension any person who is childlike) has angels that are always holding them before the face of the Father who is in the heavens (Matthew 18:10). *In the air you're breathing now angels are holding your face before your Father!*

We need to contemplate on this — placing ourselves with Christ in the immediate reality of God's kingdom of love — *before* suffering comes. *Once a painful circumstance hits you'll tend to react according to the beliefs and habits you already have.*

A Girl Dying of Leukemia Trusted Jesus

A physician named Daniel Foster tells a remarkable, true story about a precious little girl who trusted Jesus in her suffering and found peace. The girls' mother was very distressed and asked Dr. Foster why one of her twin girls was dying of leukemia and the other was not. He tried to help her find comfort in God, but she was agnostic. So he gave her C.S. Lewis' book *The Problem of Pain* to read, but after reading it she said, "Why did you give me this B.S. to read?"

But the young mother had a dramatic paradigm shift after an experience with her daughter. This girl had never been taken to church or Sunday school and had never been told about Jesus Christ. As she lay dying, suddenly she turned to her mother sitting by the bed and said, "Mother, who is Jesus?"

And the mother replied, "He was a great man, a wonderful teacher."

The little girl asked, "Do you like Him, mother?"

And she replied, "Yes, I like Him very much."

Later the little girl spoke again, "Do you see Him, mother?"

"See who?" the mother replied.

And the little girl said, "Jesus. He is standing at the foot of the bed. Do you see His crown, mother?"

She replied, "No, honey, I can't see it."

Then the little girl said, "He is calling for me, mother." And with that she died.

The girl's mother and the nurse who were present reported that this happened at dawn on a very calm day and yet at the moment the girl died there was *a sudden great rush of wind* heard outside the house and then it turned calm again.

After the risen Christ appeared to her dying daughter the mother became a Christian and joined Dr. Foster's church![52]

The God Jesus Knows as "Abba"

If it weren't for Jesus we wouldn't know that God is our Abba. Perhaps we wouldn't even know God as Father, as there are only a few references about this in the Old Testament. Thankfully, Jesus not only spoke of God as a loving Father and taught us to pray to him, "Our Father," but he demonstrated the tender and affectionate Abba Father heart of God. And because of this our

New Testament is full of inspiring and healing verses on the Father's love for us.[53]

"Abba" is one of our most precious names for God! It's maybe the best name for describing the heart of God. Abba is the Hebrew word for "Pa-pa" or "Da-da," the very first words that come from the mouth of a little Jewish boy or girl. It ought to bring a smile to our face and warm our hearts to pray to God as Abba! It did for Jesus. Probably he often talked with God as his Abba.

What a great blessing
to pray to God as Abba!

We know that in Jesus' time of great need in the Garden of Gethsemane, just before he spilled his blood for us, he cried out to God again and again like a little boy calling on his Abba (Mark 14:36). He is showing us here and throughout the Gospels — and the Apostle Paul elaborates on this — that God desires for us to know him as our Abba (Romans 8:15, Galatians 4:6).

Consider the Lord Almighty, the King of kings... The Creator of the heavens, the earth, and you and me... The God who flung the stars in the sky and calls them each by name... The Lord who makes the clouds his chariot and whose voice is like the sound of thunder...

He's the Trinity of Father, Son, and Holy Spirit to whom all the angels in heaven bow as they sing, "Holy! Holy! Holy! Is the God who was, who is, and who is to come."

He's the Lord God who shines like the sun and is so awesome and glorious that whenever anyone in the Bible encounters him in a vision or hears him speak they fall to the ground trembling, completely undone...

This Sovereign Lord God says: "You can call me 'Da-da.'"

Da-da. God wants us to know that the youngest, most vulnerable, most needy part of you and me is welcome in his arms. He wants us to find safe refuge in his loving embrace. Because he knows that in order for us to live in his abundant life and to share this life effectively with others we need to trust him.

So when I meditate on the Easy Yoke Gospel I like to pray, "Thank you, *Abba,* Lord of heaven and earth..." And in The Apprentice Prayer sometimes I pray, *"Abba,* I adore you" and "Dear *Abba,* I ask you to ordain the events of this day and use them to make me more like Jesus..."

If I know God as my Papa and trust he's ordaining events — not *causing* bad things, but *sanctifying me* beforehand and *redeeming what's bad* afterwards — it helps me to trust him.

Having pleasant circumstances is nice, but being Christlike is an eternal blessing!

Jessica Trusted God as her Abba

Jessica's mother didn't believe her. She was alone with the "dirty secret" of her father's abuse until she took courage and told me everything.

I believed Jessica. I spent many hours listening to her cry, question, scream, or be completely unable to speak. I sat with her week after week as she trembled, hid her face in her hands, and told her story, little-by-little. It was a long healing process for her. She had many losses to grieve. She needed to be healed of shame. She needed to recover her dignity, her voice, and her ability to say no. She needed to learn to forgive and trust again.

For a long time Jessica couldn't "forgive" God. Her image of God was damaged and distorted. She saw the compassion of Jesus in the Gospels and she trusted him, but *she didn't trust God.* God is a father and fathers were not to be trusted! Furthermore, while she saw Jesus in the Bible, she didn't think he was present in her life because he didn't stop the abuse.

Learning to trust me, a man, as her therapist and then looking to me as *Christ's Ambassador* helped Jessica to heal her image of God. Prayerful meditation on healing Biblical imagery was also important. For instance, Psalm 91 gives a picture of God as a loving mother and Jesus' Parable of the Prodigal Son gives a portrait of God as a Father who is compassionate, generous, and sacrificial (Luke 15:11-32).

Jessica also needed to receive the ministry of healing of memories prayer. This helped the little girl in her history and in her heart who was frozen in fear and muted by shame to connect with God's love. Through being guided in a prayer process she took the hand of her inner child and led her to Jesus and through him she came to trust God as her Abba.

To experience God as your caring and kind Papa you need to approach him from the posture of the child inside of you. This is where growing up in Christ begins (Ephesians 4:22, 1 Peter 2:2). It includes *renouncing* false narratives like "Don't be needy" or "Don't be emotional." Then it's safe for the little boy or girl in your heart to come out and receive empathy from a Christ's Ambassador. This is the *supernaturally normal* way for the Lord to heal and redeem your hurt into a "sacred wound" that draws you closer to God and enables you to minister his love to others who are hurting.

Experiment

Being Childlike

Brennan Manning, an author beloved by hurting people who are seeking God, writes to draw us closer to the God that Jesus knew personally as Abba:

It can be unequivocally stated that the central, most important theme in the personal life of Jesus, the theme that lies at the very heart of his revelation, is his growing trust, intimacy and love of his Abba, his heavenly Father. The interior life of Christ was completely Father-centered. The master clue for interpreting the gospel narrative, the foundation of Jesus' compelling demands, the source of his towering zeal was his personal experience of God as Abba.[54]

Indeed, Jesus shows us the Abba Father love of God in the way he treats children:

[Jesus and his disciples] came to Capernaum. When he was in the house, he asked them, "What were you arguing about on the road?" But they kept quiet because on the way they had argued about who was the greatest.

Sitting down, Jesus called the Twelve and said, "If anyone wants to be first, he must be the very last, and the servant of all."

He took a little child and had him stand among them. Taking him in his arms, he said to them, "Whoever welcomes one of these little children in my name welcomes me; and whoever welcomes me does not welcome me but the one who sent me" (Mark 9:33-37).

Now watch what happens just a few days after this lesson on welcoming children:

People were bringing little children to Jesus to have him touch them, but the disciples rebuked them. When Jesus saw this, he was indignant. He said to them, "Let the little children come to me, and do not hinder them, for the kingdom of God belongs to such as these. I tell you the truth, anyone who will not receive the kingdom of God like a little child will never enter it." And he took the children in his arms, put his hands on them and blessed them. (Mark 10:13-16).

The disciples could've helped these children to connect with Jesus. They could've blessed them, but instead they shooed them away as if they were a nuisance, as if the Master was too busy with "more important things." *By rejecting the children they rejected Jesus!* (Matthew 25:40, Luke 9:48).

So the Lord rebuked his disciples again and warned them that they would miss out on the Father's world if they didn't *learn from children and become like them.* This was a shocking teaching! In their day people viewed children as *possessions.* Even in our socially advanced society it wasn't long ago that we said with impatience, "Children are to be seen, not heard."

But Jesus says for everyone to hear: "Bring the little children to me!" He cuddled with them, played with them, and loved on them. Jesus was sharing with the children (and adults like you and me!) the love of his Abba.

Recall Jesus' prayer for the humble and childlike that opens our text: "Thank you, Father, Lord of heaven and earth. You've concealed your ways from sophisticates and know-it-alls, but spelled them out clearly to [little children]."

It's Time to Play with Jesus!

As a child I remember knocking on the door of a neighbor friend and asking, "Can you play?" It always felt like a risk. I was being vulnerable — I knew he might say no. But usually he said yes and that little question from my heart led to games of catch, fishing expeditions, walking to 7-11 to get a Slurpee, messing around in the field, catching frogs, and all kinds of fun!

Let's do an experiment to bring out the child in you. This week set aside your work and normal responsibilities for a time and say to Jesus, "Can you play?"

Thank you Jesus! Even now I bring the child in me to you and your Abba.

Let me suggest five ways that you might do this. I've done them all a number of times! Maybe you're willing to try one this week? You may feel silly, but ask Jesus to help you bring the childlike part of you to Abba. *Trying new experiences with God is an important part of how we heal emotionally and grow spiritually.*

1. *Skip with Jesus!*

   Find a sidewalk or a long hallway and start skipping as you exclaim, "I'm Abba's child! I'm Abba's child!" It'll make you happy. It'll make you feel loved. You're using your body to engage your mind and heart in being God's child. (It's okay to do this exercise where no one can see you!)

2. *Sing to God like a child!*

   Sing songs of thanks and praise to God (in church or by yourself) and use your hands to express your worship (using your hands will help to express your love for God with thoughtfulness and affection). Make up your own hand motions like kids are taught to do in Sunday School.

3. *Find a happy picture of Jesus.*

   Google a picture of Jesus laughing or playing with children. Sit on the floor (little children are on the floor a lot!) and imagine being a child and enjoying Jesus. Smile — better yet, *laugh!* — with Jesus.

4. *"Heart" Jesus.*

   Go to a beach and draw a huge heart in the sand and write in it, "I love Jesus!" Or you can do this with chalk on your driveway or back patio.

5. *Color a picture for Abba.*

   Color a picture to express your desire to be free and childlike in your love for God as your Abba.

"Greet God with a childlike "What's next Papa?" (Romans 8:15, MSG).

A Breath Prayer From the Bible

"My skin screams to be touched!" a recently divorced man cried to me. His embodied soul was desperate for Abba's embrace. There's a yearning like this in all of us. But we cling to people. We try to impress them. We rush around and strive to succeed. We worry. We accumulate more and more stuff. We live for exciting experiences. We escape into entertainments or alcohol.

O, my friends, Jesus shows us the Abba Father love of God that we yearn for! Being embraced by Abba is the treasure of the Kingdom of God. Nothing else will satisfy our souls!

I was reminded of my longing for Abba during a time of extended solitude and silence on an "Embracing Abba" retreat that my wife Kristi and I helped to lead. As I walked through the gardens on a beautiful spring day I prayed a favorite Breath Prayer I learned years earlier from going on retreat with Brennan Manning: "Abba... I belong to you."[55]

As I prayed this I looked to Jesus to help me know and trust God as he does. This became a prayer of my heart: "Jesus... Embrace me in Abba's love." And it led me on a journey of "Inner Child Prayer." Let me share it with you.

Imagine yourself as one of the children with Jesus in a Gospel story (e.g., Matthew 18:2-5, 10-14; Mark 10:13-16)...

Picture what you looked like when you were little and what your personality was like...

Recall a time when someone helped you to connect with Jesus and his Abba when you were a child...

Recall a time when someone made it harder for you to see and trust God as a loving Father...

Ask the Shepherd of Souls to help you trust God as your Abba... See him smiling with his arms open to you... He shows you that God is your loving Father... Take a deep breath... Relax in the arms of Jesus, your Lord and Savior... Trust your Papa...

Pray, "Jesus... Embrace me in Abba's love."

Soul Talk

When we share with a friend or small group our hurts, longings, or what Christ is teaching us it helps us to trust Abba.

1. What is one thing that you learned about trusting your Heavenly Father and his kingdom?

2. What aspect of God's love is hardest for you to trust? What is an example?

3. What helps you to be childlike before God? For instance, how did it affect you to pray, "Jesus... Embrace me in Abba's love"?

Five

Thinking God's Thoughts About You

Twenty-five years ago when I was studying to become a psychologist I had to practice giving counseling sessions in front of a one-way mirror. Behind the mirror was my professor, who was holding a clipboard to make notes on how well I offered empathy, made interpretations, and was helpful to the client. Huddled around the master counselor was my whole class of graduate students in training. *Everyone was watching me!*

The client was an 18-year old young woman just starting out as a freshman in college. It had to be difficult for her to share her life story and emotional struggle with a "rookie" counselor and to do so in front of a whole class of onlookers! (That was the price she paid for a free therapy session.) But I was so anxious about having *my* performance scrutinized that I had trouble tuning into her feelings — it's no wonder I didn't get very good marks from my teacher!

Receiving "constructive criticism" in front of my peers (so they could learn too) was embarrassing. I felt like a lousy therapist. My head dropped and my shoulders drooped as I thought to myself,

> Who are you kidding? You don't even know how to show good empathy, let alone guide the counseling session in a helpful way. Why are you wasting the best years of your life and tens of thousands of dollars to get a Ph.D.? Just give it up. Surely, you misunderstood God's calling on your life and he has something else for you to do.

Thankfully, I got help with these self-criticisms (and accusations from Satan) so I didn't quit studying to become a psychologist. Decades later, I'm still blessed to live out 2

Corinthians 5:20, my Life Verse, by serving as "Christ's Ambassador" to people who are hurting or struggling.

To get free of condemnation I had to learn how to *change classrooms,* to walk out of the one-way-mirror-room and into a one-way-Christ-room! Making Jesus my Teacher, instead of my own internal critic, has brought me the grace and truth I've needed (John 1:14, 17). As my friend Bobby Schuller says, "I'm a happy student of Jesus!"[56]

Let's step into Jesus' Kingdom classroom and be his happy students for life!

"I'm Not a Good Enough Christian"

I am one of many people who admire Kristi as beautiful, wise, compassionate, and very capable. She's an incredible wife, mother, psychotherapist, and co-founder with me of our Soul Shepherding ministry to leaders. She's the loveliest servant of Christ on earth! Yet, she's in a one-way-mirror-room too.

For instance, as we were raising our three children (who are now each in high school or college — wow, those years went fast!) Kristi often felt bad about herself as a mother. She compared herself to other Orange County, CA moms and felt inadequate. Kristi would tell me things like,

I don't fit in with the women at the kids' school or at church. They're so attractive, intelligent, and generous. It's no wonder they don't invite me to things and don't really want to know me.

I hear about other moms taking their kids to music lessons, soccer, and scouts and I feel bad that I only let our kids be in one activity at a time — *that's all I can manage!* But look at Joanne — she does all those things for her kids and she does such an amazing job of leading the Awanas program at church. Recently she had all the kids over to her house. She served them healthy snacks and made it so fun for everyone. She got them in groups by their teams and she helped them make the cutest team banners. Each team picked a Bible verse and each child made a felt doll of themselves with yarn hair and eyes that matched theirs, team uniforms, and a little piece of sports equipment — even the boys enjoyed doing it.

I can't do that! I'm not that creative and organized. I just don't have the energy. I'm overwhelmed with just taking care of our three kids, the house, and working part time. Some days I'm doing good just to get out of bed!

Even worse were the times that she *plummeted into self-hatred.* She'd cry out to me from her quicksand:

I'll never be good enough! I need to be better and to do more, especially as a mother, but I'm just weak and lazy. My kids are suffering because I'm not doing enough for them.

And the worst part is that I've let God down; I'm disappointing Him! I'm not a good Christian and I'm sure not a good witness for Christ. I'm afraid that I'm burying my talent and God is angry with me.

How is Your Self-Esteem?

How about you? What is your concept of yourself? Try this test to help you better understand how you view yourself. Answer each question below with "yes" (mostly true for you) or "no" (mostly *not* true for you). Then circle each "yes" answer:

1. When I look in the mirror I tend to focus on my faults.

2. When I do a job I usually think I should have done it better.

3. I do not feel I have much to offer to other people.

4. I feel guilty about sins from my past.

5. I often compare myself to other people and come up short.

6. When I speak in front of people I am self-critical.

7. I often worry that other people think badly of me.

8. When I make mistake I tend to get frustrated with myself.

9. I do not feel that I have much to be proud of.

10. I get frustrated about my weaknesses.

11. When I do not succeed at something I feel inadequate.

12. When I have a conflict with someone I feel it is my fault.

13. When someone shows me positive attention I feel unworthy.

14. I think more about my negative traits than my positive ones.

15. I often criticize myself.

16. There are things that I do not like about myself.

17. When someone is angry with me I feel bad about myself.

18. I do not like myself when I get emotional.

If you have five or more yes answers (or any that are painful for you) then you need help appreciating your belovedness.

Worm Theology

If you struggle with feeling bad about yourself then when someone criticizes you it can be devastating and demoralizing because *it's two against none!* Your own internal critic and the observer behind the one-way mirror are ganging up on you. To make matters worse, your condemning self-evaluations may be "baptized" by misinterpretations of Scripture.

Many Christians who struggle with self-condemnation have a "worm theology." They believe that the Bible teaches them to think of themselves as worms. They feel eligible, even deserving, of being talked down because they accept negative messages like:

• "I'm not significant." (Or "I'm not beautiful.")

• "It's prideful to think highly of yourself."

• "My heart is wicked and deceitful" (Or "I'm just a sinner.")

• "I should feel guilty."

- "I messed up so I have to make up for it."

These negative messages are *a heavy, painful yoke to bear!* They evoke anxiety, guilt, and shame. Careful Bible study shows that these are false narratives, they're "Biblical Blunders that Bruise and Confuse!"[57] Worm Theology is not Biblical!

When the Psalmist cries out, "I am a worm and not a man!" he is not giving a theological statement on the nature of people, but is describing his personal feelings of humiliation over being persecuted (Psalm 22:6).

When Jeremiah writes, "The heart is deceitful above all things and beyond cure," he is not saying that your heart is *all bad* — he's directing us to look to the Lord to deliver us and fill our hearts with true knowledge (Jeremiah 17:9).

Or when Paul teaches, "I know that in me (that is, in my flesh,) dwells no good thing" he is contrasting his natural self that is corrupted by separation from God with his Christ-redeemed self that relies on the Holy Spirit (Romans 7:18, KJV).

Christians who view God as devaluing or condemning them are projecting onto God their own self-criticisms, which originated from their pride and emotional wounds. *Shame takes us away from love and mercy and bullies us into hiding.* It's from Satan, the father of lies (John 8:44) and accuser of God's people (Revelation 12:10) — it must be rebuked!

Shame is a bully. Cry out for God to fight for you!

We Need More than Self-Love

Our typical Christian answer to low self-esteem is something like: "You are special to God so love yourself. He created your personality and gave you gifts so you can achieve great things." It becomes a self-help project of trying to raise our own self-esteem (or get God to do it for us). But our Teacher warned us all, serious students and curious crowds alike: "Anyone who intends to come with me has to let me lead. You're not in the driver's seat; I am... Self-help is no help at all. Self-sacrifice is the way, my way, to saving yourself, your true self" (Mark 8:34).[58]

There is no doubt that *God delights to bless us in every way,* but Jesus and the Bible show us a counter-cultural approach to self-esteem. The Bible directs us to focus not on self-improvement, but on *God-worship.* Proper self-love is a natural byproduct of loving God. But when we go directly after self-esteem, even using Bible verses to get it, it eludes us. We're invalidating the promise because we're not in the right posture to make use of it!

Self-love and self-help don't satisfy.
Jesus' way does: *love God and one another.*

The wonderful blessings that the Bible offers us are always associated with living in submission to God's kingdom rule. We can't make them come true for ourselves.

Jesus' yoke *binds* us to his leadership, his work, his way. Then in time we discover that being in the Lord's yoke as his apprentice is the best and most blessed life possible! It is from *inside the yoke* that we're finally able to rest in God's grace which has been there for us all along.

It's in this posture of submission to God that the Psalmist marvels, "The glorious Lord Almighty is mindful of me! He cares for me! He crowns me with his glory! Everywhere I go he is there thinking of me with concern and saying that I am precious to him."[59]

Jesus elaborated on this, indicating that the Father's care for us is so intimate that he even counts the hairs on our heads! (Matthew 10:30). There is no doubt: *God is thinking of you with love right now!*

Delighting in the Lord Who Delights in You!

Our easy yoke Savior says, "Come to me. Get away with me and you'll recover your life." He offers to us the peace that he's experiencing personally. He's just been rejected by three cities but he doesn't get discouraged, instead he goes right to prayer and celebrates God's sovereignty and finds delight in his Father's love.

Jesus is showing us that to recover our life we need the renewed self-image that comes as we delight in the Lord who delights in us. The Bible teaches, "Delight yourself in the Lord and he will give you the desires of your heart" (Psalm 37:4). Ask yourself, *Am I delighting in the Lord who delights in me?*

This is the true source of self-esteem: *Loving the One who is Love and finding ourselves cherished by him.* (Love one another relationships in Christian community are part of this.)

But if you're not appreciating God then his love isn't getting through to you. Jesus could be in the flesh beside you showering you with his kindness and mercy, but if you're not looking at him, listening to him, and trusting him then it won't do you any good.

Perhaps we're thinking so much about our deficiencies or our projects that we *miss the opportunity to think about God and the beautiful things he is already doing in our lives.* In other words, if we haven't gotten rid of our internal critic then it'll deflect the grace-messages that God communicates to us. How tragic it is when our own harsh self-judgments and unrealistic self-expectations render God's love for us ineffective!

As Paul taught, "Those who trust God's action in them find that God's Spirit is in them — living and breathing God! Obsession with self in these matters is a dead end; attention to God leads us out into the open, into a spacious, free life" (Romans 8:6-7, MSG).

Being self-critical is a form of anxious obsession on self. We need to take the internal critic off the throne of our heart and adore the God of grace!

Being self-condemning is a form of anxious obsession on self.

Ray Ortlund taught me to make *enthusiastic* worship of the Lord my number one priority in life. It's the most important thing we can do! (After all, it's the first of the Ten Commandments that God gave us!) I spent hundreds of hours talking with Ray in small group, on retreat, and over private lunches and in every single conversation I found myself drawn to delight more in God and give more of myself to serve him. Ray explained:

Worship is the highest and noblest act that any person can do. When [people] worship, God is satisfied!... And when you worship, you are fulfilled!... We who were once self-centered have to be completely changed so that we can shift our attention outside of ourselves and become able to worship Him...

Worship is top priority. Everything, absolutely everything, must be set aside to do this...

A person may say, "Well, I just don't get anything out of it."

You get nothing out of it?! You get nothing out of the Word of the eternal God?! You get nothing out of the great hymns of the church?! You get nothing out of prayer through Jesus Christ to God Almighty?!

That's because you don't know how to put anything into it. It shows our deep misunderstanding of what worship is all about... Worship is the meaning of the whole thing of living.[60]

To worship God all we need to do is to put our minds on him. We readily become God-absorbed when we meditate on Scripture or the wonders of creation. God's goodness and beauty naturally draw us in to give thanks to him, sing his praises, devote our lives to him, and love our neighbor in Jesus' name. *What joy is ours when we think deeply on the Lord!*

God alone is the balanced Person. God the Father, God the Son, God the Holy Spirit — they alone are really whole. God alone is sufficient in Himself. We have been so constructed as His people that we are only whole, we are only sufficient when all our lives are revolving around Him. We must be God-centered![61]

And when we are God-centered we start reflecting God's glory! "Those who look to him are radiant; their faces are never covered with shame" (Psalm 34:5).

If you're self-critical you're an open target to be shamed. Shield yourself in Christ!

In Christ

We've been praying, "Lord Jesus, I seek to live as your apprentice in all that I do today." That's an identity. We're taking on "the mind of Christ" (1 Corinthians 2:16). We're seeking to assimilate his mind — his ideas and attitude — into our *whole person,* which is why in The Apprentice Prayer we say: "My Lord, I devote my whole self to you. *I want to be all and only for you, Jesus!* Today, I seek to love you with all my heart, all my soul, all my mind, all my strength, and all my relationships." (We're praying to love God with each of the dimensions of our person that Jesus references in the Great Commandment from Mark 12:30-31.)

To take on Christ's mind means that we're formed by the words of Scripture as he was. He learned to pray from the Psalms and often quoted them (Luke 24:44). He realized his identity as Messiah by studying the prophecies of the Old Testament (Luke 24:25-27). He got his life mission statement from Isaiah (Luke 4:18-19, Isaiah 61:1-2). He acted to fulfill the Scriptures (Matthew 26:54). He became the Word made flesh (John 1:14).

The Apostle Paul urged us, "Let the word of Christ dwell in your richly" (Colossians 3:16). Similarly, he prayed for us "that Christ will be more and more at home in your hearts as you trust in him" (Ephesians 3:17, NLT). He knew that receiving Christ into our heart-dwelling was the beginning of growing into God's way of abundant living.

But he wanted us to grow beyond receiving Christ *in me* and see that Christ was welcoming us into *his home,* to live with him in his way and for his glory and to be a blessing to him and to other people in his name. We're invited to live *in Christ!*

Being in Christ is the key to your life. Again and again the Apostle Paul implores us to live in Christ, which is to say in effect, "Devote yourself to living as Jesus' apprentice. Get caught up in his life from above." He lives this way himself, boasting, "I glory in Christ" (Romans 5:17). In fact, in his epistles he refers to our position "in Christ," 160 times![62]

- In Christ we are a new creation (2 Corinthians 5:17).
- In Christ we become God's children (Galatians 3:26).
- In Christ we have every spiritual blessing (Ephesians 1:3).
- In Christ we have the forgiveness of sins (Ephesians 1:7).
- In Christ we are God's masterpiece (Ephesians 2:10).
- In Christ we have glorious riches (Philippians 4:19).
- In Christ we are rooted and built up (Colossians 2:7).

- In Christ we gain an excellent standing and great assurance (1 Timothy 3:13).

What a *blessed yoke!* Oh to be *in Christ!* I want him to be my "first love" (Revelation 2:4), "the center of [my] life" (Philippians 4:7, MSG), the "one thing I ask" (Psalm 27:4). I want to sit at his feet and love him as Mary of Bethany did (John 12:1-8). I want to give up all things to follow him (Luke 9:24). I want to give him that drink of water he's thirsty for (John 4:7).

Kristi Was Saved From Self-Hatred!

But to *experience* our blessed identity in Christ *we need more than Bible verses we also need the loving care of people in the Body of Christ.*

It's the grace-yoke of life in Christ that saves us from self-hatred. As Kristi has grown in this life she has found further healing from guilt and shame. She followed the same advice that we tell the people we counsel and mentor: *"You'll receive help when you and I join God in caring for you."*

To receive help join God and a
soul friend in caring for you.

I love the way Aelred of Rievaulx (1110-1167) said it many centuries ago:

Here we are, you and I, and I hope that Christ makes a third with us. No one can interrupt us now, no one can spoil our friendly conversation; no one's voice or noise will break in upon this pleasant solitude of ours. So come now, dearest friend, reveal your heart and speak your mind. You have a friendly audience; say whatever you wish. And let us not be ungrateful for this time or for our opportunity and leisure.[63]

Over time in her conversations with me, a counselor, a mentor, and her spiritual friends Kristi internalized the nonjudgmental love of God into her heart in new ways. By sharing herself honestly with people she felt safe with she drew from God's grace and displaced her internal critic. In the same way, we all need a few Christ's Ambassadors in our lives to help us stay connected to the God of grace (2 Corinthians 5:20).

Kristi was surprised to learn that her self-condemnations were a form of *pride or self-reliance;* she had been cutting herself off from God by saying that she wasn't good enough to be loved by him, that his mercy wasn't enough for her. Unwittingly, she was diminishing her appreciation of God's greatness and hindering the flow of his grace and peace into her soul. Her self-focus left her in guilt and shame, powerless to effect her freedom.

Learning continually to re-direct her thoughts and feelings onto God was essential for Kristi. *She needed something to hold onto so she wouldn't sink in the quicksand of self-deprecation: the Word of God became her solid lifeline.* There are many ways she's been doing this: memorizing passages of Scripture like Romans 8 (see below), meditating on God's promises (like the ones above), and recalling to her mind how whenever anyone in the Bible asked the Lord for mercy he gave it.

For instance, Brennan Manning, one of Kristi's favorite authors, illustrated that Jesus is "the Deliverer from self-hatred through love" by healing Mary Magdalene from her shame and isolation:[64]

> Magdalene was awed by the loveliness and compassion of this magnetic man. His eyes had called out to her, 'Come to me. Come now. Don't wait until you have your act cleaned up and your head on straight. Don't delay until you think you are properly disposed and free of pride and lust, jealousy and self-hatred. Come to me in your brokenness and sinfulness with your fears and insecurities and I will comfort you. I will come to you right where you are and

love you just the way you are, just the way you are and not the way you think you should be.'

Jesus had convinced her that "winter had passed, that the rains were over and gone" (Song of Solomon 2:1), that her sins had been forgiven and that God now accepted her and approved of her. The moment she surrendered in faith, love took effect and her life was transformed. The result was the inner healing of her heart manifested as peace, joy, gratitude and love... The creative power of Jesus' love called Magdalene to regard herself as He did, to see in herself the possibilities which he saw in her.[65]

Jesus accepted Mary Magdalene before she became his disciple.

Manning says that like Mary Magdalene, we can't heal ourselves from self-hatred, anxiety, or any of our problems:

I cannot free myself. I must be set free. Jesus... invites me to make friends with my insecurities, smile at them, outgrow them in patient endurance, live with the serene confidence that he never abandons his friends, even when we disappoint him...

Jesus says: that is the way my Father is. He wants you home more than you want to be home. His love knows no bounds. Never compare your pallid, capricious, conditional human love with my Father's love. He is God not man.[66]

Another way that Kristi used Scripture to re-direct her thoughts onto God was to use the Jesus Prayer: "Lord Jesus Christ have mercy on me."[67] To this day when critical thoughts ambush her and throw her down into feeling bad about herself Kristi says,

I take my feelings of failure and inadequacy and I confess those to the Lord. Then I pray the Jesus Prayer slowly over and over till I sense that I've received his mercy. This focuses me on the cross and Christ being enough for me — it stops my self-criticism. It becomes okay that I'm not enough because Christ is and he gives himself to me — he is what I really need!

Kristi also has learned to stay out of self-hatred by *incarnating for others God's word of mercy.* When feelings of shame start to come upon her she focuses on something good that she can do for somebody else. She explains,

It helps to distract me from my feelings of worthlessness if I serve somebody in a position of obvious need. In this way I get my eyes off of myself and am able to participate with God in serving somebody else out of love for him. This is not about denying my needs or earning God's favor — it's about getting in the flow of God's grace.

If none of these ways work, and I'm really stuck in feelings of shame then I turn on worship music and start praising God. That always helps.

Scripture Memory

As you go about your day what do you think about? Every moment of every day you and I have the freedom to think about *whatever we want.* The thoughts that you choose to dwell on are a key factor not only in how you feel, but also what you say and do and ultimately the person you become.

The way to overcome anxious thought patterns like self-criticism (or any negative attachment for that matter) is with a positive connection to God. Memorizing Scripture and then using it for meditation and prayer is an indispensable way to engage our minds, and ultimate our whole person, with God. I know of no better way to re-direct worries than to put my thoughts on God's Word and then let the Holy Spirit use the Scripture to teach me and draw me into greater intimacy with God.

With the Word of God revealed to me as the risen Christ I have the divine Counselor and *Friend* that I need. I can then let go of the Worry Witch and embrace the Prince of Peace.

When you memorize Scripture you're taking its structure, wisdom, and grace inside your mind. Once its life-giving insights and inspirations are in your thoughts and feelings then they can get into your heart to form your will and permeate your body, social interactions, and the flow of your soul's personality.

The Proverb is true: "As a person thinks in their heart that's who they become" (Proverbs 23:7, paraphrased). And when you hide Scripture in your heart (Psalm 119:11) then you can take it with you wherever you go so that at any time — while driving, waiting in line, brushing your teeth, or laying in bed unable to sleep — you can mull over God's Word and let it lead you in prayer.

"We live at the mercy of our ideas."
Dallas Willard

Memorize *Loooong* Passages

The typical approach to Scripture memory is to memorize lots of individual verses or short passages on topical themes. This is a helpful approach for learning key doctrinal points, witnessing for Christ, and using simple meditations like Breath Prayers.

But few Christians memorize whole paragraphs or chapters of the Bible. This dramatically *deepens* our experience with God's Word! It's powerful for our spiritual formation in Christ to drink from the flow of Living Waters that's in the Bible. It naturally leads us to meditate and pray — we simply let the Holy Spirit carry us along, renewing our minds in the goodness and wisdom of God that's revealed in his words.

Martin Luther taught that to memorize a section of Scripture and then call it up for prayer is like carrying around a *pocket lighter* to warm you up to God's presence. In his pastoral letter to his barber he wrote:

> A good prayer should not be lengthy or drawn out, but frequent and ardent. It is enough to consider one section or half of a section [of God's word] which kindles a fire in the heart. This the Spirit will grant us and continually instruct us in when, by God's word, our hearts have been cleared and freed of outside thoughts and concerns...
>
> With practice one can take the Ten Commandments on one day, a Psalm or chapter of Holy Scripture the next day and use them as a flint and a steel to kindle a flame in the heart.[68]

Another important aspect of memorizing long passages of Scripture, rather than only verses, is that it forces us to *submit to God's Word*. We tend to try to make the Bible say what we want it to say! But it's harder to take Scripture out of context when you take it in through long passages.

The thought of memorizing a whole chapter of Scripture might be intimidating to you. Just don't start with Psalm 119, the longest chapter in the Bible! Instead start with Psalm 23 or another one of the "electric passages" of Scripture.[69] Memory is like a muscle so if you start small and keep exercising your mind you'll be surprised by how much Scripture you can memorize!

Mostly, Scripture memory requires *repetition over time*. Repeating words over and over brands them into your brain, especially as you concentrate and seek to understand what you're reading. Seeing insights and connections in the passage will help you to remember. Also, your memory will be greatly aided if you use visual images for themes and acronyms for lists.

Be Renewed in Romans 8

"Be transformed by the renewing of your mind," Paul teaches us (Romans 12:1). God's Word diagnoses (Hebrews 4:12), washes (Ephesians 5:26), and gives life (Genesis 1, Matthew 4:4) to our minds and ultimately our whole being when we memorize it, study it, meditate on it, and pray through it with an open heart, applying it to our specific needs.

A powerful chapter to memorize and one that is particularly helpful if you struggle with feeling bad about yourself is Romans 8. It begins and ends by reinforcing the blessings of being "in Christ" and all throughout it is full of God's gracious promises. Here God teaches us how to *tap into the electric current of his Spirit that raised Jesus from the dead!* (Romans 8:11). *Eighteen times* the Holy Spirit is named in this one chapter, where as he is only named ten times in the other fifteen chapters of Romans combined.

Romans 8 is filled with Holy Spirit
dynamite to elevate your mind and body!

The eighth chapter of Romans was key for helping Kristi to fill her heart with God's grace. She was meeting with Jane Willard (Dallas' wife) for some healing prayer sessions and Jane suggested that Kristi memorize Romans 8. Kristi recalls, "I read it and re-read it. I read it in every version I could find. I read commentaries and asked people about what it meant, but it seemed so hard to understand and so impersonal. For me it was dry, wordy, confusing."

But Kristi printed out Romans 8 on a sheet of paper anyway. She carried it with her for a whole year, memorizing it little-by-little." She reports,

> As I memorized it then *it came to life for me* and became very personal, healing, and beautiful. I began to experience the truths of Romans 8 that overcome my feelings of self-hatred: I'm not under condemnation. The Father has chosen me and justified me. I've been given the spirit of adoption and the Holy Spirit testifies that I'm God's child and helps me with my weakness. Jesus is the only one who has the right to judge me and he is interceding for me. So nobody can bring any charge against me! *Nothing can separate me from God's love!*

Kristi says, "I'm not a real studious type of person so if I can memorize Romans 8 then I bet you can too!"

But you may want to pick a different section of Scripture since it took her a whole year to memorize such a long and complex chapter! There are two other ways that you can squeeze the juice out from Romans 8. You could memorize my condensed version that includes key verses[70] or you can meditate on these "Romans 8

Promises for Disciples of Jesus," putting your name in each one and proclaiming it out loud:

• There is no condemnation for _____, who is in Christ Jesus (v. 1).

• The Spirit has set _____ free from sin and death (v. 2).

• The Spirit who raised Jesus from the dead lives in _____ and is energizing _____ (v. 11).

• _____ is led by God and thus is a child of God (v. 14).

• _____ can call God "Abba" or Daddy! (v. 15).

• Through Christ _____ is an heir of God, inheriting divine blessings (v. 17).

• _____'s body will be redeemed, set free and made whole (v. 23).

• The Spirit helps _____'s weaknesses with intercessions from deep inside (v. 26).

• All things work together for the good of _____ who loves God and is called according to his purpose (v. 28).

• God takes initiative to know, guide, call, justify, and glorify _____, helping _____ to become more and more like Jesus (vv. 29-30).

• If God is for _____ then who can be against _____? (v. 31).

• In all things _____ is more than a conqueror through Christ's love (v. 37).

• Nothing — absolutely nothing! — can separate _____ from the love God that is in Christ (v.v 38-39).

A Breath Prayer From the Bible

Ask God to lead you to one of the Romans 8 Promises to meditate on. You may want to paraphrase it to use it as a Breath

Prayer. For instance, based on verse 1: "In Christ... there is no condemnation for me." Try it this way:

- Slowly breathe in the wonderful words of your blessed position before God: "In Christ..."

- Hold your breath and your Lord sweetly in your heart...

- Exhale and release any feelings of guilt or badness: "There's no condemnation."

Or here are some other options for using Romans 8 verses as Breath Prayers:

- "Holy Spirit... Set me free!" (v. 2).

- "Spirit of Christ raise me up... Forever" (v. 11).

- "Abba... I belong to you" (v. 15).

- "God is for me... Who can be against me" (v. 31).

- "In the love of Christ... I'm a conqueror" (v. 37).

Soul Talk

One of the ways that as students of Christ can renew our minds in his word (message) is to through soul talk.

1. What are you learning about how living in Jesus' easy yoke of mercy sets you free from self-condemnation?

2. Do you criticize or condemn yourself? What is an example?

3. This week how has putting your thoughts on Scripture helped you to connect with God's grace through Christ?

Six

Hurry Up to Be Still

I was running late to a seminar at church and so I was in a hurry. The lady in the car in front of me started slowing to a stop right in front of me. "Why is it always when I'm rushing that I get behind a slow driver?"

Then the light started to turn red — *I raced through.*

I got to my left turn and the sign said: "No left turns from 6:30 am to 9:00 am." It was 8:35 am. I turned left anyway. *I'm almost there. Five minutes late and counting!*

Approaching the parking lot there was a stop sign. Nobody was around so I looked both ways, rolled through it, and parked. As I got out of my car it hit me: *I just broke three traffic laws and I'm going to a "Lead Like Jesus Seminar!"* I slunk my way into the church hoping that no one would recognize Pastor Bill!

Then, as if that wasn't enough conviction, at the seminar Ken Blanchard stressed the importance of Christian leaders slowing down their pace and putting margin in their schedules. I knew that God was talking to *me!* To influence people for God like Jesus did I needed to make more *space* and *slow down!*

Back then I often relied on adrenaline to keep a fast pace. And when I slowed down and didn't do anything "productive" for an extended period of time, like when I was on vacation, I felt restless, bored, empty, and depressed (the symptoms of adrenaline withdrawal).

But at that seminar the Lord was drawing me into a slower, quieter, and less driven life by wooing me into the delights of a more intimate relationship with himself!

Always Late

Stories like that seem to help Type A pastors feel like I can relate to them! Kent is an example. One day he was ten minutes late for his meeting with me, as usual. He tried to make a joke of it, "I'm sorry. I guess I need 25 hours in my day!" Invariably he ran late for meetings and events because he was always trying to squeeze one more thing into his day.

Kent complained about having too much to do and being tired of rushing around all the time. He thought his hurried, overcrowded life was inevitable for him as a pastor who had a family and lived in Orange County, CA in the 21st Century. But being an adrenaline addict in recovery myself, I knew better! So I spoke the truth in love to him, "I think you like being in a hurry and doing so much. Maybe the feeling of urgency and importance energizes you."

My friend disagreed with me. But the night before his next therapy appointment he had a dream that he took his wife and two girls on a picnic. As they walked along he was carrying the picnic lunch and the lawn chairs and his wife was holding the hands of their little girls. And he led his family to sit down together *on the fast lane of the freeway!*

So there they were trying to enjoy their picnic lunch while cars kept racing by! The cars had to slow down and move out of the fast lane in order not to hit them! But then a truck came barreling down the freeway, close behind a car, and not seeing his family sitting there, it was about to run them over!

That's when Kent woke up — in his nightmare a*nd in his life!* After processing his dream with me he admitted, "You were right in what you said to me last week. I am going way too fast. My wife has been trying to tell me the same thing."

Kent's conversations with me and the readings I gave him helped him to become more aware of how much he was using adrenaline to stay *keyed up.* He began to realize that he was *choosing* to fill up his calendar and to race from thing to thing and his hurried lifestyle was keeping him from enjoying God's peace and being more attentive to people in his life.

To experience God's peace we need to be *unhurried*.

To be sure, from time to time Kent had sought to be nourished by the God of Peace, like on extended family vacations or spiritual retreats. But it would always take him a long time to enter into a relaxed state of being and once he returned to his daily responsibilities he would go right back to his hurried self.

"Get Keyed Up!"

Kent had what medical doctors call "hurry sickness." I showed him the underlying attitudes that perpetuated his hurried and harried approach to life:

- "If you don't hurry you're going to miss out."
- "Don't waste time."
- "Multi-tasking is essential to success."
- "Get excited!"
- "24 hours in a day isn't enough for all I have to do."
- "I shouldn't have to wait on anyone."

These phrases surge with adrenaline! Dr. Archibald Hart believes that "adrenaline dependence" has become the greatest addiction problem in America today. You can actually become "hooked" on the energy, pleasure, confidence, and power that come when your body's stress hormones of adrenaline and cortisol are released.[71]

God has designed our bodies wonderfully and it is a great gift that we have this instinctive, adrenal "fight or flight" response to danger and other emergencies. Adrenaline alerts us to grab our child's hand at the curb when a car races by. It gives us confidence when we are doing an important presentation. It energizes us when we need to overcome a challenge or work through a conflict. It cushions us when we get bad news.

We need adrenaline to handle real life emergencies, but we may use it to get "keyed up" with feelings of confidence and control for daily life situations.

- Pastors may use adrenaline to get up for their sermon.

- Business people use it to get through a 60-hour workweek.

- Parents may depend on it to get their children from one activity to the next.

- Students who study late into the night use it to stay alert while depriving themselves of sleep.

Using a modest amount of adrenaline to face challenges like these is natural and good — as long as we then return to a calm state. But we may seek spikes of adrenaline, along with extra coffee or other caffeinated drinks, to help us stay in "top form."

Fast-paced, high-energy living is admired and rewarded in our society, perhaps especially so in our Christian culture.[72] In fact, in my twenties I used to justify my hurried, adrenalized lifestyle by (mis)quoting from the Bible: "Redeem the time for the days are evil" (Ephesians 5:16, KJV).

I didn't realize that I was damaging myself. I was abusing my body's speed chemicals to boost my ego. I was putting my health at risk of stress-related illness. I was repressing underlying feelings of depression and emptiness that needed to be dealt with. I was making it harder for myself to hear God's voice. Worst of all, *I was rushing past love.*

Do you use adrenaline to avoid feeling depressed?

Do You Have Hurry Sickness?

It's not just Type A's that get hurried — less ambitious personalities may get sucked into fast-paced, distractible living. I find that many people who are over-relying on adrenaline don't know it. This self-test can help you to see if you might be susceptible to hurry sickness. Answer each question with "yes" (mostly true for you) or "no" (mostly *not* true for you). Then for each "yes" answer circle the number on the left column.

1. Are you often in a hurry, rushing from one thing to the next?

2. During a typical day do you work with intensity on something that seems urgent?

3. Do you tend to do two or three things at once to be more efficient?

4. Are you productive, busy, or active almost all the time?

5. Do you regularly rely on caffeine to feel energetic and focused?

6. If you're not working on something do you rely on stimulation from activity, entertainment, or noise?

7. When you're resting do you feel fidgety, pace, drum your fingers, tap your feet, or chew fast?

8. If you're idle do you feel guilty or restless?

9. When you're waiting are you usually uncomfortably impatient (e.g., looking at your watch, getting upset, or counting items in the short order line)?

10. When you go to bed at night do you typically think about all the things that you didn't get done and need to get done?

11. When you go on vacation do you feel empty, bored, or depressed?

12. Do you often have physical stress symptoms like gastric distress, rapid heartbeat, headaches, muscle pain, teeth grinding at night, and sleep problems?

If you have four or more yes answers you may be depending on adrenaline (and other stress hormones like cortisol) to manage daily life.

Love Is...

If you were asked, "What is love?" How would you answer?

Many people think love is a desire or a feeling and that's why we say, "I *love* chocolate cake!" But really *we just want to eat it!* When love is degraded into *mere desire* it's no wonder people "fall" in and out of love so easily.

Other people know better and define love as choosing to care for others. But very few of us would define love as the Apostle Paul does when he writes, "Love is patient..." (1 Corinthians 13:4).

Why *patience?* Why does Paul indicate that love begins there? We show our resistance when we joke, "Never pray for patience!" Maybe my fresh wording for patient love can help us:

> Love endures and suffers long with people; it is not easily irritated or impulsive. Love moves *slooooowly* — it is *never in a hurry* and it is always willing to wait. Love sets aside time to notice other people. It takes time to thank God for the wonders of his creation all around us.

My friend Alan Fadling in *An Unhurried Life* makes the point that taking time — *not being in a hurry* — is the path of Love.[73] Paul defines love by focusing on patience because all the other attributes of 1 Corinthians 13 love depend on patience.

If we're in a hurry our ability to love is compromised. All the expressions of love that you can think of — listening, doing a kindness, offering a compliment, giving a gift, forgiving a sin, or praying for someone — require time. It takes time to pay attention to others and what they need and then to respond with kindness.

Moving at a *relaxed pace* — not trying to do too much, too fast — gives our soul the space it needs to breathe in God's Spirit. As we connect with the God *who is love* then we receive his blessing and power to be compassionate, kind, and generous toward others.

Love is unhurried.

When I was young I was told to read 1 Corinthians 13 by putting my name in there: "Bill is patient. Bill is kind..." But I can't do that and neither can you! That mentality generates pressure to measure up or guilt about falling short. Even if you seem to succeed for awhile you'll be relying on your self, not on God, and thus you'll be feeding pride.

It's Love (with a capital "L"!) that is patient and kind. So we need to first read 1 Corinthians 13 by putting the name of the Lord in there first: *"God* is patient with me. *God* is kind to me..." As God's love lives in us through the Spirit of Christ then we will naturally be able to share his love with others (1 John 4:16, 19).

That's Jesus' Good News Gospel! We can grow in the grace of God. We can count on the kindness of the King. This is a much better narrative for our lives than, "Hurry up or you'll miss out!"

"Just a Tekton"

Most of Jesus' earthly life seems "wasted" in obscurity. He lived a quiet life in a small town, working as a "Blue Collar Worker." Apparently, he didn't give any notable sermons or perform any healings or make any disciples. Nobody even had an idea about who he was except Mary. This was the Father's plan and Jesus followed it.

Have you thought much about Jesus' quiet, humble years in Nazareth? Why was the Son of God tucked away in a hick town working as a common laborer? He looks great at age twelve debating the religious leaders in the temple! If we were in charge we'd say, "Send him out! He's ready and the world needs him!" But the Father has him wait... And wait... For *eighteen more years!*

Then when Jesus finally does launch his public ministry his family and friends in his hometown of Nazareth don't believe in him and reject him, despite his miracles and astounding wisdom. They say, "How could this be? Jesus is just a carpenter! We saw him grow up. We know his family" (Mark 6:2-3, paraphrased).

The Greek word for Jesus' trade is "tekton." We translate it as "carpenter" but it can also be "stonecutter," which was more likely since there was lots of stone in Israel, but not much wood. Another hint comes from the archaeological digs of the ancient city of Sephorris, which is just over the hill from Nazareth. In Jesus' day Nazareth was a small village with not many jobs, but Sephorris was a heavily populated and wealthy city with lots of opportunities for tektons. Dating back to the time of Christ there was a beautiful outdoor stone amphitheater and expensive homes. You can see these things today.

Imagine Jesus as a tekton laborer.

Jesus surely visited the enormous theatre that was so close to his home and maybe he helped to build it! We know that to describe the Pharisees he took the word "hypocrite" or "play actor" from the world of theatre.

"Jesus may have been a tekton laborer," I said to the bi-vocational pastors in Mexico that Kristi and I minister to. They work fifty hours a week on construction sites or in factories for $2 an hour and pastor their neighborhood churches in evenings and weekends. They could easily identify Jesus doing "sweat work" and being treated as low class.

Picture the Nazarene carrying large rocks on his back to the job site as the hot sun beats down on him. He cuts and sands the rocks into shape and places them in the theater. A wealthy boss is yelling at him to work harder! But he keeps laboring at his job to provide for his family after his father has died.

Or maybe Jesus helped to build the mosaic tile floors that have been excavated in the homes from ancient Sephorris. Imagine him on his hands and knees getting all scraped up as he puts small stone tiles in place to build a beautiful and intricate mosaic on the floor of a wealthy person's house. The owner stands over him and spits in his face, "What did you do there? You stupid tekton! That's not where I wanted the birds to be in the picture! They're supposed to be over there!"

"Yes, sir!" Jesus replies with sincere respect and a warm smile. "You're right. That will look much better. I'll fix it right away."

Or if Jesus was a carpenter probably he served customers by making things out of wood like cutting boards, bowls, chairs, and tables. Visualize him learning the trade from his father, cutting and sanding wood with his hands. Think about him serving customers who are difficult to please. Or see him loaning out his handmade tools to other workers and sometimes they're damaged or not returned, but still he's generous to share.

Jesus of Nazareth grew in the grace of giving to those who asked of him. He loved his neighbors. He loved his enemies and he blessed those who cursed him.

Even during his public ministry the Son of David often returned to hiddenness: withdrawing to be alone with the Father, taking the role of an ordinary servant, keeping his miracles secret, limiting himself to a human body, not pushing an agenda on people.

Jesus did hard labor with love for God and his neighbors. He did mundane and menial work with cheerful praise to God. He was mistreated by people of worldly power and wealth and yet he was kind to them. He endured two decades of seemingly being set aside and forgotten as insignificant. He lived a cross-carrying kind of life even in his hidden years. So when you and I experience these trials we can see that the tekton Jesus is already there loving us and inspiring us.

Being "Just a tekton" was Jesus' badge of honor.

Jesus' Quiet, Loving Service

As with Jesus' hidden years, many of the ways he loved people get overlooked; they slip through the cracks in our attention as we read the Gospels.

For instance, look how graciously our Lord treats people who intrude on his space and interrupt him. (In fact, if you removed all the "interruptions" from Jesus' ministry we'd lose huge chunks from the Gospels.) People crowded around him, pulled on his robe, kept begging for what they wanted, yelled at him from the other side of the street, stopped him when he was walking somewhere, set children at his feet when he was trying to preach a message, chased after him when he went away for solitude and prayer, or peppered him with questions. But Jesus didn't view these people as bothersome — he patiently cared for them.

Or consider the ways Jesus quietly served people. He repaired broken chairs. He fixed breakfast. He washed feet. He touched lepers. He healed sick people. He played with children. He listened to the broken-hearted. He went to parties with social outcasts. He invited the poor into the Kingdom of the Heavens. He loved his enemies, blessed those who cursed him, and prayed for those who persecuted him. Day after day for three years he quietly taught a few uneducated men and women how to be his apprentices in kingdom living.[74]

How did Jesus love so patiently and kindly? How did he resist temptations to use hurry and control to get his own way?

He trained himself to live in God's presence at an unhurried pace — first in Nazareth and then in his public ministry. For instance, often he waited with the Father in prayer early in the morning before he ministered to people in the Gospels, and surely he did the same thing during his many years in Nazareth. He practiced waiting. He learned patience and kindness.

Jesus waited patiently in God's easy yoke. How do you feel about waiting?

The "Little Way" of Love

Jesus taught us to follow his way of loving servanthood. It was a main theme in his teachings:

Do your good deeds in secret... Whoever wants to be great must become the servant... The first shall be last and the last shall be first... Blessed are the merciful... Give and it shall be given unto you... Give a cup of cold water... Feed the hungry, care for the sick, visit those in prison... Wash one another's feet... Welcome little children... Love your enemies... Bless those who insult you... Pray for those who persecute you... Give away your coat... Go the extra mile... As you do unto the least of these so you've done unto me.[75]

Richard Foster explained how Thérèse of Lisieux[76] (1873-1897) in her short life followed Jesus' example of humble service:

This Little Way, as she called it, is deceptively simple. It is in short, to seek out the menial job, to welcome unjust criticism, to befriend those who annoy us, to help those who are ungrateful. For her part, Thérèse was convinced that these "trifles" pleased Jesus more than the great deeds of recognized holiness.

The beauty of the Little Way is how utterly available it is to everyone. From the child to the adult, from the sophisticated to the simple, from the most powerful to the least influential, all can undertake this ministry of small things. The opportunities to live in this way come to us constantly, while the great fidelities happen only now and again. Almost daily we can give smiling service to nagging co-workers, listen attentively to silly bores, express little kindnesses without making a fuss.[77]

Serving God in the Little Way doesn't get much attention. Most people would rather do great things for God and be applauded by large crowds. But simply giving cups of cold water in Jesus' name adds up. It lends dignity and hope to the needy and it works to conquer our own selfish ambition and pride.

Like Thérèse, we can learn to follow Jesus into this Little Way — *but only if we first imitate the way he slowed down to appreciate the Father and abide in his love in the moment.*

Unhurried With Jesus

In a busy, hectic season of life and ministry Pastor John Ortberg called his mentor Dallas Willard and asked him: "What do I need to do to be spiritually healthy?"

There was a long pause and then Dallas replied, "You must ruthlessly eliminate hurry from your life."

John then asked, "What else should I do?" (It seems he didn't like the first answer!)

After another long pause Dallas answered, "There is nothing else."[78]

The priority of being unhurried was built into the temple in Jerusalem. When I visited the site and walked the same south entry steps that Jesus walked on I noticed that the steps were irregular — they varied in length, some being long and others being short. I learned that this was done on purpose to slow people down as they came to worship! Walking slowly helps us to be more attentive to God.[79]

"Noble people are known by the way they walk."[80]

Imagine if we slowed down like that in our churches today! Sadly, most of us rush into church five minutes late and distracted! But in these pages we've been enjoying Jesus' Easy Yoke Message of "Walk with me in my unforced rhythms of grace." He's saying, "Be unhurried with me." It's rarely preached today but it's a common theme of his in the Gospels:

- Slow down and listen... Whoever has ears to hear, listen...

- Calm down your thoughts... Who of you by worrying can add a single hour to his life?...

- Walk with me in the light (don't run in the dark) so you don't stumble...

- Peace! Be still...

- Come away with me to a quiet place and rest...

- Stop your busy work to sit at my feet and listen to my words...

- Watch and pray... Be constantly alert... Keep praying...

- Wait for my Father's gift of the Holy Spirit...

- Take time to love your neighbor...[81]

Jesus lived by his own teaching: he was never in a hurry — *except to go the cross and die for us!* When the Father said it was time he turned and headed straight for Jerusalem, leading his disciples with great resolve (Mark 10:32 and Luke 19:28). If we stay yoked to Christ then our only hurry will be to listen to God and obey him.

The one time to hurry is to listen
to God and obey his Word!

How Kent Learned to Be Still

Kent had to make a *lifestyle change* to walk in cadence with Christ's grace rhythms. He needed to re-think true "productivity" and realize that moving too fast or too aggressively was a liability, especially in ministry. It was time for him to *prostrate his productivity before the Lord!*

I told Kent he needed to "Hurry up and be still!" He needed to see that the *one urgency* for his life was learning to slow down, connect with Christ, listen to him, and follow his lead. The prophet Isaiah sounded this alarm for the harried, distracted people of his day, but they didn't listen:

> This is what the Sovereign LORD, the Holy One of Israel, says: 'In repentance and rest is your salvation, in quietness and trust is your strength, but you would have none of it. You said, 'No, we will flee on horses.' Therefore you will flee! you said, 'We will ride off on swift horses.' Therefore your pursuers will be swift! (Isaiah 30:15-16).

A place for Kent to start in his plan for personal formation in the unhurried yoke of Christ was practicing the discipline of adding margin to his schedule. He needed to open spaces in his day to breathe and connect with the Lord and to practice times of being still and waiting before appointments. Gradually this *changed his body chemistry to be less adrenalized.* He was beginning to experience the "real rest" of Matthew 11.

Experiment

Statio (Enjoying a Selah)

In the 11th Century a Benedictine monk named Gerbert invented the mechanical clock for calling people to stop working and to pray. In the next few centuries the machinery was perfected and mass produced so that clocks were in more and more places throughout society. Eventually they became watches that people carried with them. People's experience of time became fixed and portable, whereas previously it'd been flexible and closely tied to the natural, gentle rhythms of the sun. Increasingly, time became a way to measure productivity, first in business, then in seemingly every area of life.

Today in our technological age we live with an astronomical pressure for speed, efficiency, and output. We've lost our sense of time as sacred. We've lost margin. We've lost space to be unhurried and to relate. We've lost *life.*

The Benedictine monks continue to ring their church bells and call us to pray. If you stay at one of their monasteries, as I've done many times, you'll find that the bells ring ten minutes before the service starts to give you time to walk from your room or the garden to the chapel and arrive early to pray before the prayer service starts! They call this "statio" ("sta-ti-ō"), which is Latin for station.[82]

Many of my work days are full of meetings so practicing statio's spiritual margin is an extremely helpful discipline for me. Waiting *on purpose* stops my productivity mode and helps me to recollect myself in God's presence here and now. It's an opportunity to pause, breathe deeply, and pray that I and the people I'll be with will join what God is doing in our upcoming meeting, event, or activity. Of course, it also helps us to show respect and consideration for other people's time. It's applying

Paul's teaching to humble ourselves and consider others as better than self (Philippians 2:3).

Statio is the spiritual discipline of arriving early
to meetings and events in order to pray quietly.

Sometimes, for one reason or another, I neglect statio and I'm running late. What then? Do I hurry or go into self-condemnation? No. I can still be unhurried in my *attitude* and pray as I transition to that next engagement.

One reason I used to be late all the time was because I hated waiting on people! I'd get so impatient and frustrated with feeling disrespected and time being wasted, but really *I was the one wasting time because I was missing the opportunity to enjoy God and to pray for the person who was late.* (Of course, you may need to set a boundary with someone who disrespects you. We'll talk about that in Chapter Eight.)

The Best Time to Be Unhurried

The best time to ruthlessly eliminate hurry may be the hardest time: *the first thing in the morning.* C. S. Lewis explains:

> The real problem of the Christian life comes where people do not usually look for it. It comes the very moment you wake up each morning. All your wishes and hopes for the day rush at you like wild animals. And the first job each morning consists simply in shoving them all back; in listening to that other voice, taking that other point of view, letting that other larger, stronger, quieter life come flowing in. And so on, all day. Standing back from all your natural fussings and frettings; coming in out of the wind.
>
> We can only do it for moments at first. But from those moments the new sort of life will be spreading through our

system: because now we are letting Him work at the right part of us. It is the difference between paint, which is merely laid on the surface, and a dye or stain which soaks right through.[83]

Are you hounded by "wild animals" in the morning? Often times I am! Lewis' admonition inspired me to begin each day in statio, slowly and serenely praying The Apprentice Prayer. Laying in the arms of Jesus is the best place to ask God to ordain the events of our day!

Dallas Willard's morning ritual for setting aside "fussings and frettings" and "letting that other larger, stronger, quieter life come flowing in" was to linger in bed while luxuriating on Lord's Prayer and Psalm 23.

Experiment With "Selah"

The word for margin or statio in the Bible is *Selah*. 72 times the Psalmist prays or sings, "Selah" — *often right in the middle of a sentence!* Selah probably means, "Pause to reflect in prayer."

Selah is the restful disposition of the Psalmist when he prays: "But I have stilled and quieted my soul; like a weaned child with its mother, like a weaned child is my soul within me" (Psalm 131:2). Selah is an *unhurried space* to listen to God; it's a breather to help us appreciate God's loving presence. (It's occurred to me that perhaps selah is the sound of breathing in, "Se" ["say"] and breathing out, "lah." You might try this now!)

To experience selah-rest in your daily life you need to identify some concrete ways of practicing statio. For instance, meditating on Jesus' prayerfulness, patience, and kindness like we did earlier made me think, *Maybe I should welcome the yellow lights instead of pushing through?* So I actually made it a spiritual discipline out of appreciating red lights! Even at stop signs I come to a full stop and often I'll take a deep breath and pray, "Thank you Lord for stopping me!" I'm enjoying the Selah-yoke of Christ.

It's good to slow down for Selah in the evenings, which is encouraged in many of the Psalms (like 3, 4, 62, 127, and 130). This is a natural time to rest and reflect on your day.

"The *stops* of a good person, as well as their *steps,* are ordered by the Lord." George Muehler, 19th Cent.[84]

If you're used to moving fast and being highly productive then statio will be difficult for you! Any restless energy in your body or racing thoughts in your mind will resist slowing. You'll probably feel the urge to pick up your smart phone!

Also if someone else is late, making you wait, you may feel irritated! Confess your emotions to God. Then think about how often you've made people wait and confess this lack of consideration to God and thank God for his mercy to you. This will help you to share God's mercy with those who are late by praying for them and being gracious.

Learning something new is supposed to be difficult so don't worry about it! *You're training.* Keep practicing making spaces in your schedule, taking prayer pauses, finding opportunities to breathe in and out: "Se... lah..."

This week ask Christ to help you be in his unhurried yoke. Here are some experiments to try for enjoying *Selah:*

1. When you wake up linger in bed to meditate on a Scripture.

2. Leave early for an appointment and use statio time to wait on purpose and pray before it starts.

3. Schedule statio breaks in your day and use them to take a breather in prayer.

4. Move some things from today's to-do list onto tomorrow's.

5. Turn off your smart phone or TV and sit quietly for awhile.

6. Drive in the slow lane and meditate on Jesus' words, "The first shall be last and the last shall be first."

7. Walk s-l-o-w-l-y from one place to the next. Feel the sun, see the flowers, hear the birds, and say hello to people!

8. Contemplate in Psalm 46:10. (See examples below.)

Be Still as the Lake at Dawn

One morning I was enjoying a Sabbath day for prayer and I was reciting and praying through Psalm 46 as I walked around the lake near our home. I was particularly drawn to the words God spoke to the Psalmist: "Be still and know that I am God" (v. 10). I meditated on different translations of the verse to draw out nourishment for my soul, like a bee sucking nectar from a flower:

- "Step out of the traffic! Take a long, loving look at me, your High God" (MSG).

- "Our God says, 'Calm down, and learn that I am God'" (CEV).

- "Cease striving and know that I am God" (Dallas Willard's paraphrase).

- "Quiet your heart, rely on me — the Spirit of Christ, the I AM — living and breathing in you" (my paraphrase).

We sing these "Be still" words as if they're a lullaby. We print them with serene pictures as if they belonged in a peaceful monastery. These are fine meditations, but the words "Be still" are far more than pretty words — *they're powerful!* The Psalmist is finding peace in God while dealing with storms, earthquakes, tidal waves, collapsing governments, and nations at war!

God is teaching us to look beyond the visible, stressful circumstances and see into the invisible Kingdom of the Heavens in our midst where, "There is a river whose streams make glad the city of God... [Here] the Lord Almighty is with us; the God of Jacob is our fortress... [He is the one who] makes wars cease to the ends of the earth" (vv. 4, 7, 11, and 9).

As I was meditating on Psalm 46 that morning the noisy traffic nearby beckoned me to hurry and get to work — I had a lot to do! At the same time the quiet lake and the Word of God called out to me: "Be still and know that I am God." Enjoying Selah inspired my creativity and I composed a prayer poem:[85]

> *Be Still*
> Be still as the lake at Dawn
> In a world that wakes to alarms and agendas:
> Quietly rest so you can listen;
> Breathe and open to your soul;
> Wait patiently to receive what is to come,
> Softly absorb the light as a looking glass.
>
> Be still to know the I AM;
> Let the "rush hour" pass by your silence:
> The Voice whispers to create Life;
> It swims and plays deep within you;
> As holy feet step upon your waters
> Heaven's Face smiles upon you
> — and out from you.

A Breath Prayer From the Bible

If you tend to hurry, don't like waiting or feeling unproductive, or struggle with anxiety then it's especially important to practice statio. By setting aside generous spaces of *un-stressful and un-hurried "quiet time"* for Scripture meditation and contemplative prayer you're teaching your body to calm down and pray God's word: "Be still..."

Being at peace in God's presence will empower you to love others well, serving Christ in the Little Way that is the mark of genuine love.

Praying God's word to "Be still" trains us to live peacefully in the Selah-yoke of Jesus!

Relaxed, deep breathing is such a help to me and many of the people I work with. Especially when combined with meditation on Scripture, deep breathing helps us to slow down an antsy body and jitterbugging thoughts. It's a way of relying on the Holy Spirit within you to help your mind to focus on God and your body to be still in his presence. You're heeding Jesus' call to "watch and pray" with him; you're training with the Master and asking him to help you learn to become the kind of person that when stresses come you do not react with worry, agitation, impatience, or trying to control things, but you remain in God's peace.

Let's use Psalm 46:10 to practice this now:

- Breathe in deep and slow as you think or whisper: "Be still and know that I am God..." (It takes a long, sloooow breath — you may need to practice this!)

- Hold your breath as you appreciate God's Word of peace...

- Then breathe out and *relax in God's presence...*

- Repeat this pattern a few times...

Then you can try my "Simplifying Breath Prayer," using one breath in to pray each line:

- Be still and know that I am God...

- Be still and know that I AM...

- Be still and know...

- Be still...

- Be...

Soul Talk

We're so overloaded with information in our world that it's easy to pick up the habit of hurrying when we read! (Maybe you've been doing that with reading *Easy Yoke!?*) Certainly there are times to skim, but that kind of reading isn't likely to do much for your soul. The best learning actually comes from *re-reading* something that's been valuable for us. Lingering over these Soul Talk questions and sharing them with a friend is a way of taking a Selah to "Hurry Up and Be Still."

1. What is one thing that you're learning about Jesus' unhurried way of love?

2. Do you tend to be in a hurry? Rely on adrenaline to get keyed up? Get so busy that you don't enjoy the moment? Run late for meetings?

3. What impact did it have on you to practice statio? How was it for you to pray "Selah" or "Be still" from Psalm 46:10?

Seven

Working With Easy Yoke Power

"How are you?" my friend Steve Harper asked me on the phone.

"Busy," I replied.

"What else is new?" he laughed. "Ever since we roomed together in college I've admired how disciplined and productive you are!"

That was the year 2000. I realized then that I was *too busy*. I was driven to be ultra "productive," always trying to do more in less time. I stayed up late *and* woke up early. I shaved with my electric razor while I drove to work. I routinely scheduled appointments back to back to back. I worked through lunch. I worked on Sundays. I worked in the office, at church, at home, and in my yard. I carried a heavy sense of responsibility everywhere I went. I didn't relax much. I didn't smile enough.

If you had gotten inside my head back then you might have heard anxious chatter that sounded like this:

> I have to finish preparing for the class I'm teaching on depression tomorrow. I don't want to just "wing it" and do a bad job like last time, but when am I going to find time do that? I have a full day of therapy clients. On my lunch break I need to go through my list of messages and call people back — I don't feel like it, but I better because these people need help and besides I'm short on clients and we're under budget this month. Oh, and tonight we're going to Kristi's parents' house to celebrate David's birthday. After that I'll work on my talk — but that means I won't have time to exercise tonight or be able to go to bed when Kristi does...

"More is Better!"

I feel tired just remembering that heavy yoke! But it seemed I couldn't help working all the time. Looking back, I can see I was trying to compensate for feeling inadequate inside. The combination of my anxiety to prove myself to be worthy, along with my enormous capacity for work, made me a workaholic.[86]

You don't have to be a workaholic to have a problem with overworking or worrying about the things you need to accomplish. Perhaps you stress about having enough money or getting your errands done or finding just the right outfit or preparing a good dinner for your family. Or you might find yourself trying too hard to help someone you're concerned about. *But the non-anxious yoke of Jesus is the source of true productivity!*

I find that pastors, leaders, and caregivers are especially prone to stress overload from doing too much. What about you? What does it sound like inside your head? Maybe you think:

- "I have to prove myself."

- "If I'm going to succeed it's up to me."

- "If you want something done right do it yourself."

- "I can't rest till my work is done."

- "I should always be doing something productive."

- "Idle hands are the devil's workshop."

- "I need to do more."

Thought patterns like these may drive you to accomplish more, but are they true and good?

Are You Overworking?

You may not consider yourself a "workaholic" and yet you may have some issues with working compulsively. This test will help you to see if maybe you overwork or relate to your work in unhealthy ways. We're looking at "work" in the broad sense. Work is not just paid employment; it is also things like projects you're doing, responsibilities you have, chores you complete, volunteer service you give, and ministry you offer.

Answer each question below with "yes" (mostly true for you) or "no" (mostly *not* true for you). Then circle each "yes" answer:

1. Do you find that you are able to work on a job or a project longer than most people?

2. Do you keep thinking about things you're working on during free moments or while going to bed?

3. When you're interrupted in the middle of a project do you get irritated?

4. Do you feel restless or guilty if you're not working on something?

5. Do you get so focused on your goal that you don't enjoy the process?

6. Do you put yourself under pressure with self-imposed deadlines?

7. When you're not accomplishing something productive do you feel inadequate?

8. Do you take on more than your share of responsibility because you don't want people to think poorly of you?

9. In the last two months has working long hours hurt your family or friends?

10. When you don't succeed do you feel bad about yourself?

11. Do you put more thought and energy into your work than your relationships?

12. Do you tend to take on more work than you have time for?

13. Is your work the thing that excites you the most?

14. Are you easily frustrated when your work is not going well?

15. Do you need to succeed at what you're working on to feel significant?

If you have four or more yes answers then you may be working compulsively. If you have eight or more yeses then you may be a workaholic, using work to cope with unwanted emotions and needs and at risk of stress overload or burnout. (Before my renewal I think I had yes answers on all 15 questions!)

Workaholism is working lots of hours to self-medicate or for ego reasons.

Why Do We Overwork?

Even as I write to you about the easy yoke of Jesus I am in danger of slipping out it myself! So I keep reminding myself to take my own words to heart, to take breaks from writing and to pray and rest in Christ while I write.

Blaise Pascal, the great French mathematician, scientist, and Christian theologian of the 17th Century, poignantly described our problem with restless activity and overworking: "All the unhappiness of people arises from one single fact: *they cannot stay quietly in their own room.*"[87]

Why not? Why can't we stay quietly in our own place? Why do we overwork or stay so busy even when we know better?

Being preoccupied helps us to avoid feeling things that we don't want to feel. When we are still and quiet any inner distress that we are experiencing naturally rises to the surface.

We need to understand that problematic overworking is more than just working too many hours — it's also *working for emotionally unhealthy reasons.* Most of us work "too much" for particular seasons and may do so for good reasons. The problem is when we overwork *continually* or when we do our work with the *pressured mindset* of "I have to prove myself."

Underneath the workaholic's compulsion to work are feelings of guilt, inadequacy, emptiness, or fear (like fear of disapproval or not having enough money). Overworking is a compensation that attempts to "get rid of" those painful emotions.

When we overwork to prove ourselves or to feel better we're relying on ourselves without the assistance of God's grace, we're trying to secure ourselves apart from the divine domain. Always the Lord is at hand to bless, guide, and empower. But when we're determined to put our nose to the grindstone and get the work done we don't see the risen Christ there with us. All we need to do to tap into God's mighty power is to stop relying on our own muscles and be like the little leper who mumbled to Jesus, "If you wanted to you could heal me" (Matthew 8:2, paraphrased).

Pressuring ourselves to do more is an unbiblical script for life that generates anxiety and can render God's grace ineffective in our lives. It's a *heavy yoke* to wear! It's nothing like "walking freely and lightly" in "the unforced rhythms of grace" that go with the Easy Yoke Gospel.

God-Ordained Work

Many Christians make the mistake of thinking that work is part of God's curse that came with humankind's fall into sin. But *work actually is part of God's original intention for us in the Garden of Eden.* When God created us in his image he commissioned us to work and to be productive by *relying on his leadership and blessing* (Genesis 1:26-28).

Work is good and necessary for life and community. Work can be defined as whatever we do that produces something good and beneficial for others. Managing a grocery store, selling real estate, waiting on tables in a restaurant, or any other honest and decent job is an opportunity to *serve other people in love.*

So what is the curse? It's working in the wrong way, *working "by the sweat of our brow"!* (Genesis 3:19). Jesus redeems us from cursed work by teaching us how to pull the plow of work in his easy yoke. When we work *with him* and *in his way* our work is holy and healthy and we won't experience stress overload or burnout.

It's not work that is cursed, but "sweat work."
Jesus' easy yoke undoes the curse of the Fall!

Remember Martin Luther's letter to his barber answering his question on prayer (from Chapter Five)? In what's become a classic little devotional book he suggests something we wouldn't expect a prayer master to say:

> It may well be that you may have some tasks which are as good as or better than prayer, especially in an emergency. There is a saying ascribed to St. Jerome that everything a believer does is prayer and... 'He who works faithfully prays twice.'[88]

Luther understood that *Jesus worked hard,* first as a blue collar carpenter and then as a famous rabbi. He went from city to city preaching the Good News and engaging people in conversation about the Kingdom of God. He spoke to masses of people day and night, sometimes thousands at a time. His active ministry of compassion and healing fills the pages of the Gospels.

For three years Jesus lived with his apprentices 24-hours a day, investing himself in them. He encouraged them. He served them. He answered their questions. He taught them how to live and to love. He showed them how to preach, heal, and teach. Jesus worked so hard that he said of himself, "The Son of Man has no place to rest his head" (Matthew 8:20). Frequently, crowds of needy people pressed around him and his disciples. There was so much to do that *they didn't even have time to eat!* (Mark 6:30).

Paul also worked hard. He served full time discipling leaders, planting churches, and ministering to people — *and* he subsidized his ministry by making tents with his own hands (Acts 18:3). He teaches us to work hard too:

> We showed you how to pull your weight when we were with you, so get on with it. We didn't sit around on our hands expecting others to take care of us. In fact, we worked our fingers to the bone, up half the night moonlighting... We simply wanted to provide an example of diligence, hoping it would prove contagious. (2 Thessalonians 3:8-9, MSG).

As a Branch Abiding in the Vine

The key to our work is *how* we do it. What is our attitude and demeanor? Are we anxiously straining? When Type A Paul was at his best in the work of his ministry he was relaxed like Jesus. *He was drawing on easy-yoke-power.* That's what we want to learn!

Jesus taught us to be as branches abiding in a grapevine that is tended by a gardener. The sap from the vine flows into the branches so they bear clusters of juicy grapes. Jesus himself is the Vine, the Father is the Gardener, and the Holy Spirit is the life in the Vine (John 15:1-15). The point is that *the power for us to bear the fruit of love for others comes out of our intimate abiding in God.*

This is Jesus' way. He was the "Righteous Branch" who abided in God continually (Jeremiah 23:5, 33:15). He lived a life of submission to the Father — only doing what he saw the Father doing (John 6:38, 12:50). So complete was his moment-by-moment reliance upon God that he knew the Holy Spirit without limit! (John 3:34).

The True Vine told us in Matthew 11 that the fruit in his life grew out of "Father and Son intimacies" and "unforced rhythms of grace." He didn't have to push out fruit! It came out *naturally!* The powerful, life-giving Spirit-sap of his abiding in the Father's love yielded abundant, delicious fruit.[89]

Jesus' first priority was intimacy with Abba.

As we've said, Jesus lived in the abiding-yoke way as a young carpenter in the quiet and obscure town of Nazareth and as a famous preacher in the bright lights and busy days of his public ministry.

The Nazarene's abiding-in-love lifestyle flowed in a rhythm of "inner journey" and "outer journey."[90] He prayed solo and he served people. He worshiped in private and he healed the sick. He meditated on Scripture and he taught others astounding new insights. He fasted and he fed the hungry. He rested in quiet and he ministered in noisy crowds. He withdrew with Abba on retreat and he was patient with difficult people who interrupted him.

Jesus' Rhythm of Life in the Gospel of Mark

The Gospel of Mark shows us Jesus' inside-out rhythm of life.[91] Ten times Mark gives examples of Jesus going on spiritual retreat, either alone with the Father or joined by his disciples. And after each nourishing time of intimacy with Abba he shares with others the eternal fruit produced by *The Father and Son Company:*

- Jesus spends 40 days in solitude, silence, fasting, Scripture meditation, and prayer and then he launches the ministry that will change the world forever! (Mark 1:9-13).

- He goes to a "lonely place" to pray and discerns it's time to leave Capernaum to minister elsewhere in Galilee (Mark 1:35).

- Again he prays in a lonely place and *people come to him* to be ministered to (Mark 1:45).

- He keeps an all-night prayer vigil and the Father helps him decide which twelve of his large group of disciples to appoint as his apostles (Mark 3:13; Luke 6:12-13).

- He goes out for a boat ride with his disciples on the sea. He relaxes in Abba's arms so deeply that he naps through a life-threatening storm! Then he calms the storm with a word! (Mark 4:35-41).

- Again he withdraws by boat for a retreat with his disciples. Their time is cut short and Jesus feeds 5,000 with five loaves! (Mark 6:30-32).

- Our Lord climbs a mountainside to pray at night. A storm comes and he sees his apostles struggling in their boat so he *walks on the water* to come help them! (Mark 6:45-46).

- He takes Peter, James, and John high up a mountain for a retreat. He's with them, but praying in private, and then he is transfigured to shine like the sun! (Mark 9:2-13).

- With his disciples Jesus celebrates the Last Supper and then he teaches them many important lessons (Mark 14:12-31).

- He takes Peter, James, and John with him to watch and pray in the Garden of Gethsemane. Then he loves his torturers and dies for our sins (Mark 14:32-42).

In all these instances Jesus is saying, "Walk with me and work with me." He's modeling his way of resting in the Father's love and sharing this love with others. He's showing us how to abide-in-the Spirit *and act-with-the-Spirit*. He's inviting us to participate with him in the power of his Easy Yoke Gospel.

As we learn to be aligned with and attuned to God like Jesus then we too can be at peace in storms, love difficult people, have divine wisdom for life, and do miracles!

Easy Yoke Effectiveness (Optimal Stress)

The above examples of Jesus' abiding and bearing fruit rhythm of life occur in the context of *stress:* forty days of fasting, lonely places, huge decisions, dangerous storms, thousands of hungry people, apostles arguing, and crucifixion looming. Things are happening that he's not in control of. He's tempted to be afraid, discouraged, angry, depressed, or anxious. He has work to do — he's caring for and teaching others. This is his easy yoke at work!

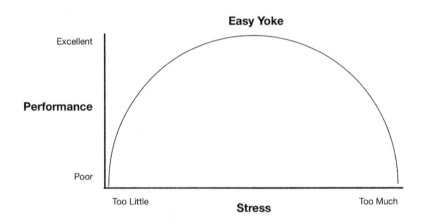

It helps us understand the power of our Lord's easy yoke if we consider the research on "optimal stress." As we saw in Chapter 3, stress is not bad, it's a natural and good part of life. *Our problem is not stress, but taking on too much or too little stress.*

As the diagram above shows, our problem with stress is having too much of it *or too little of it.* On the left side we're not stressed, we're not challenged, and we've become passive and depressed. On the right side we're over-stressed and becoming hyper and anxious. Both extremes are bad for our physical and emotional health and lead to poor performance in all areas of life, including our spirituality. To be most lively and effective we need moderate stress levels in which we're calm, alert, and engaged.

The easy yoke of optimal stress is a paradox: we work at resting in God, we wait for the Spirit and he leads us onward, we abide in Christ and bear good fruit, we humble ourselves under God's mighty hand and he lifts us up (Hebrews 4:11, Galatians 5:25, John 15:5, 1 Peter 5:6). In other words, *the easy yoke is a relaxed way of working hard* — like singing as we do a job. Anchored to Christ we're calm and happy, not straining to make anything happen, and yet we're focused and vigilant to join what God is doing.

Stay in Jesus' easy yoke and you'll get more *real work* done!

Abiding Energy

The easy yoke performs well for high-level, hard-charging ministry leaders. When meeting with church elder boards, executive teams, and other leadership groups I begin by facilitating an experience of abiding in Christ. This is more than a token devotional before "getting down to business" — it's a generous space of time designed to help leaders integrate prayer and business.

My friend Lance Wood is a Tax Partner for PwC and he also serves as a lay leader in an international ministry, a megachurch, and two missions organizations. He's busy! For years he's asked me to lead his Mexico ministry team meetings. I'll never forget the first time doing this. We were preparing to lead 120 people to care for the poor in Mexico for four days. There were lots of moving parts, lots of decisions to make, and lots of work to do. The room was full of Type A business leaders. Yet he let me carve out the first forty minutes of a two-hour meeting for meditative prayer and personal sharing! Afterwards he said,

> Thank you for leading us into such a rich time with God. It really felt to me like getting into that state of abiding before we did anything else caused us to have insights that we wouldn't have come up with on our own into how God might have this mission trip go. In business

lingo this is a best practice — we need to do it again next year (and in life!!).

Lance has come to call this "abiding energy!" Being in Jesus' easy yoke is powering his life. It's even enabled him to serve as an auctioneer and raise millions of dollars for HOPE, an amazing Christian microfinance ministry that goes into third world countries to disciple the poor to Jesus and teach them how to start their own successful businesses.

Abiding energy helps us to work smarter and more effectively. We're doing our best, but we're not trusting our best — we're trusting God. As we work or serve or whatever we're doing we're aligning with and attuning to *the presence of God in the space around our bodies.* This is what Matthew noticed Jesus doing: "Abruptly Jesus broke into prayer..."

Have you ever done this? Have you ever been listening to someone share and replied, "Let's pray about this now."?

It's easy... *Yes, Lord, God, we are eager to learn how to work with your easy yoke power in order to be more fruitful for the glory of Christ. We pray in the precious name of our Savior Jesus. Amen.*

Experiment

Sabbath

Keeping a Sabbath day is the most repeated command in the Bible — and yet it may be *the most neglected of the Ten Commandments by Christians today!*

In generations past our culture supported Sabbath. Most people went to church on Sundays and probably they got together with family or friends to share a meal, relax, and talk. Stores were closed and there wasn't much to do. Kids sports teams took the day off. If you mowed your lawn people looked at you like you were from another planet! Sunday was a special day from God to be enjoyed with God and loved ones, perhaps by taking a slow "Sunday drive" in the country, hanging out on the front porch, going for a walk, doing a Bible study, or taking a nap.

But today our culture opposes spiritual rest and God-worship. We've dismissed Moses and the Prophets who repeatedly call us to remember the Sabbath. Even we who are committed Christ-followers believe we're okay to neglect the Sabbath because we think it's not a New Testament teaching.

Actually, the Sabbath was practiced and taught by Jesus (Luke 4:16, Mark 6:1-2) and his apostles (Luke 23:56, Acts 16:13, 17:2), including those who were Gentiles (Acts 13:42-44).

What is the Sabbath? Essentially it's a fast from work, but don't think of a somber, dour fast. Think, *Fasting is feasting on God!* The Sabbath is a celebratory day in which you do no work in order to honor the Lord and be renewed by his sufficiency in your life. It's a joyful day that inspires creativity.

Eugene Peterson says that the Sabbath is a weekly day to *pray and play!* Pastors especially need this because of the spiritual and emotional intensity of their work, but many don't do it. Often they speak of their "day off," but that's a "bastard Sabbath" says the interpreter of *The Message*. Enjoying God and his blessings is different than a day to run errands or do whatever you want. Even if the activities are similar the *attitude* is totally different.[92]

Many Christians misunderstand Jesus' teachings and actions that disrupted Sabbath-keeping in his day. Yeshua was not contradicting the importance of practicing Sabbath rest to honor God; he was against the *legalistic, Pharisaical* Sabbath-keeping that was so prevalent in his day. And so he taught the people: "The Sabbath was made for people, not people for the Sabbath. So the Son of Man is Lord even of the Sabbath" (Mark 2:27-28).

Keeping the Sabbath is a *yoke* — not the binding yoke of legalism, but the easy yoke of Jesus! Our Lord made this point by breaking the rigid, restrictive rules that the religious leaders imposed on the Holy Day and healing people.[93] Far from being a duty or a chore, he made it clear that the sacred Sabbath was an *opportunity* to participate in the action of God and interact with his healing grace (Mark 7:8-13).

Pastors help people celebrate Sabbath
but when do they take a day to rest?

Living in Sabbath Rest

Some people get hung up on which day to keep a Sabbath. The Jewish Sabbath is Saturday. The early Christians made Sunday the Sabbath to honor Christ's resurrection. As the "First Day" we begin our week resting in God. But as Paul teaches, *any day* can be used for a Sabbath rest (Romans 14:4-6). That's a good thing, because Sunday is *not* a day that church pastors get to rest!

Many people also get overwhelmed with the idea that a Sabbath has to be a whole day. But practicing Sabbath rest is not all or nothing. Of course, the command itself is for a day, but we have to learn how to *become the kind of person* who keeps the Sabbath day.

So we need to *start by doing what we can to connect with God's grace*. And we need to remember, as the writer to Hebrews explains, that the point of keeping a Sabbath is not to check it off our list, but to *enter God's rest for everyday living*. This is so important that he urges us:

> Since the promise of entering his rest still stands, let us be careful that none of you be found to have fallen short of it... As was said before: "Today, if you hear his voice, do not harden your hearts."...
>
> There remains, then, a Sabbath-rest for the people of God; for anyone who enters God's rest also rests from his own work, just as God did from his. Let us, therefore, make every effort to enter that rest (Hebrews 4:1, 7, 9-11).

The Sabbath-yoke has helped me and many people I know to turn from worrying about their "to do" lists to being ruled by the peace of Christ (Colossians 3:15). To take a Sabbath is to set aside a day (or a smaller block of time) in order to rest in God's provision — to stop your work and be "unproductive." Along these lines, as Psalm 127 teaches, sometimes the best thing you can do on a Sabbath is to *sleep!*[94]

Ultimately Sabbath is an *attitude*. It means we let go of trying to run our world and we stop trying to control people and situations. You focus on what God is graciously doing all around you so you can respond to him rather than depending only on your own abilities to make things happen.

The way to enjoy Sabbath rest is to *enjoy Jesus!* In our theme Scripture he welcomes us: "Are you tired? Worn out? Burned out on religion? Come to me. Get away with me and you'll recover your life. I'll show you how to take a real rest... Keep company with me and you'll learn to live freely and lightly."

Sabbath is a day to practice resting in Jesus'
easy yoke — so you can live in it all week!

When we stop our work and rest with Good Shepherd in the green pastures of his grace and beside his still waters of love we discover that it's really true: "He restores my soul!" Then we see the right path to walk in. We're strengthened to endure difficulty. We're anointed for ministry. Our cup overflows. We dwell in the house of the Lord in all that we do! (Psalm 23).

In the grace-rhythms of Sabbath with Jesus we're set free from worry and anxiety, ambition and anger, even loneliness. Because we've discovered the reality of life in God's Great Universe: *I am not alone. Everything doesn't depend on me. Things don't have to happen my way. God is with me helping me and working all things together for my good so I can be happy in Christ no matter what!*

An Old Quaker Tailor's Example

Centuries ago the Quaker John Woolman worked in Jesus' Sabbath yoke as a tailor. He shows us the fruit of developing a demeanor of resting in God's sufficiency. He worked hard and he did good work for his customers and so his business grew. But he wrote in his journal that he was afraid that his prosperity would distract him from his relationship with Christ and staying responsive to divine "openings" in which he heard God's voice or was moved to minister God's presence to someone.

So the old Quaker never let the demands of his business grow beyond what he needed to provide for himself and his family. He determined not to worry about money and not to overwork. Instead of expanding his tailor shop, he practiced the "less is more" mentality and kept sending customers to his competitors who needed more business! How un-American! *How Christ-like!*[95]

Kristi and I first heard Woolman's story from Ray Ortlund in the early 1990's. It inspired us to be glad to refer therapy clients to other counselors who could help them rather than growing a bigger business with employees. We've carried this idea into Soul Shepherding by helping other pastors/leaders start new soul care ministries for pastors rather than grow an organization. This helps us to de-stress, shrink our egos, and rest in God's provision.

Some Ways to Practice Sabbath Rest

You may not keep a weekly Sabbath day. Personally, I learned to practice Sabbath by starting small: over a period of years I went from setting aside one day every quarter to one day per month to one day per week. *One day a week* — what a novel idea!

At first my Sabbath days emphasized solitude and silence for five hours or more, as I needed to learn to unhook from my daily responsibilities and people's expectations and to relax in God's provision. Because it is difficult for me not to be active or studious *I had to do something to help me "do nothing"!* For instance, to be still and simply *enjoy being with Jesus as my Friend* I like to take a walk with Kristi, hike, be in nature, pray the Psalms, use Lectio Divina (meditation) on a Gospel passage, journal, abide in prayer (e.g., Breath Prayers), or enjoy Christian community.

Sometimes my Sabbaths don't look so "spiritual." I've used vacation or days of relaxing with family and friends to rest in God. The important thing for me is to set aside my normal work and responsibilities one day per week. (It's helpful to pick one day that's your normal Sabbath.)

I advise you to *start small* and *be flexible* in your approach to Sabbath rest. Here are some practical ideas for how you can practice resting in God away from your work — or while you work!

1. Pray the Sabbath Psalm

Psalm 92 begins with a notation: "A Psalm to be Sung on the Lord's Day" (NLT). This seemingly forgotten Psalm is filled with vibrant metaphors and presents the Sabbath as a day to "give thanks to Yahweh" and to "play in honor of [the] Most High" (Psalm 92:1, Jerusalem Bible).[96]

2. *Sleep in*

Most people today don't get enough sleep. One day sleep *at least* eight hours or take a nap. Jesus took naps! The monks call this "napsiodivina"! If you tend to feel guilty when you're not accomplishing things then sleep or "do nothing" as a discipline to help you rest in God's grace.

3. *Abide in prayer*

Set aside about fifteen minutes in a quiet place to meditate deeply on my Psalm 62:1, 5 prayer: "In Christ alone my soul finds rest... Selah." (See below.) *Breath* to rest physically.

4. *Abruptly break into prayer*

Prepare yourself to rest in God the next time someone shares a problem with you. Instead of feeling pressure to say something helpful ask, "Can I pray for you now?"

5. *Give away business to a competitor*

If you work as a professional try following John Woolman's example of "less is more" and refer a potential client/customer to another provider who can do a good job. Put your trust in God who provides abundantly for you and enjoy the extra space of time and energy!

6. *Sing while you work*

The birds sing praise to God as they work — you can too! Sing or hum a worship song to do your work in Jesus' Sabbath-yoke. (See below.)

7. *Take a Sabbath day*

Set aside a day or a shorter block of time to rest and do no work. Don't be busy, productive, or studious. Don't fill your time with errands. *Relax. Enjoy.* Let God lead you to pray and play, to be alone or with loved ones. What would you enjoy doing with your Best Friend? *Have fun with Jesus!*

Listen to the Birds Sing

Jesus' answer to our tendencies to worry and overwork was to tell us to *look at the birds and listen!* No doubt, he did this himself and personally appreciated the birds singing so happily and beautifully as they gathered food, built their nests, and raised their young. Jesus had such a wonderful way of putting us at ease!

Don't worry about what you can get — respond to what God is giving you right now. Don't worry about how you look — open your eyes wide to God's beauty and goodness that's all around you.

Don't worry about money. Don't worry about what *you* have to do — give your full attention to what *God* is doing in your life today.

All your worrying and overworking doesn't add even a single hour to your day! Since you can't even do this very little thing why worry about the rest?

Don't worry: Look at the birds! They are carefree because your Heavenly Father cares for them. Don't you know that you are much more valuable than birds?"

Fear not little ones! Your Father has been pleased to give you the glorious riches of his eternal kingdom! Seek first his kingdom and he will provide you with all that you need (Paraphrases from Matthew 6:25-34 and Luke 12:22-34).

How many birds are you worth?[97]

The birds sing as they work because implicitly they trust the Father's care! The conversation between the Robin and the Sparrow echoes our Savior's teaching. Let's listen in with him:

Said the Robin to the Sparrow:
"I should really like to know
Why these anxious human beings
Rush about and worry so."

Said the Sparrow to the Robin:
'Friend, I think that it must be
That they have no Heavenly Father
Such as cares for you and me"[98]

Many times I've experienced the singing of the birds and thought, *There are angels in the heavens all around me praising God and ministering to me!* They inspire me to smile, skip in my spirit, or sing to the Lord. Of course, *it is the Lord himself who puts the song in our mouths* by singing with love over us (Psalm 40:3, Zephaniah 3:17[99]). It's because of the Father's love for us that we don't need to worry or overwork.

One Sabbath day I did some bird watching while meditating on Jesus' teaching on learning from the birds not to worry. As I looked and listened to what was going on above my head, Jesus spoke to my heart about being at pace in the Father's world and I wrote another prayer poem, "Don't Worry: Listen to the Birds":

Don't worry: Look at the birds;
Trust my Father as they do,
Feeding each day from his hand.

Don't worry: Listen to the birds;
Rest in my Word as they do,
Sitting quietly and alone on the Branch.

Don't worry: Learn from the birds;
Sing with my angels as they do,
Harmonizing with the choruses of heaven.

Don't worry: Live like the birds;
Fly with my Spirit as they do,
Responding to the currents of my Breath.

Don't worry: Love like the birds;
Gather with my friends as they do,
Traveling in formation as my flock.

A Breath Prayer From the Bible

In The Apprentice Prayer we say, "Today, I depend on you Holy Spirit, not my own resources. Help me to keep in step with you." This means training to step out of the world of performance pressure and to step into Jesus' world of Sabbath grace. Recall that 160 times in his letters the Apostle Paul shows us that our identity, meaning, and joy are *in Christ* alone!

Let's pause to take a breather in the arms of the Lord *now*... Refresh your soul in Christ... Fix the thoughts of your heart on Christ alone as your source... Pray slowly, "In Christ alone my soul finds rest... Selah." (Inspired by Psalm 62:1, 5.)

As you inhale focus on trusting Christ... As you hold your breath focus on keeping Christ in your heart... As you exhale pray "Selah" and focus on letting go of stress... Repeat this...

As in the previous chapter, you can try this as a "Simplifying Breath Prayer." This helps you to truly seek *only Christ!* Pray each line with a breath until all that you pray is "Christ":

- In Christ alone my soul finds rest... Selah

- In Christ alone my soul... Selah

- In Christ alone... Selah

- In Christ... Selah

- Christ...

Use Your Imagination
Imagine being like Mary while you pray "In Christ Alone." She set aside her kitchen work and her sister Martha's expectations and just *sat at Jesus' feet adoring him and listening to him* (Luke 10:38-42). Like her, set aside your work and your thoughts of

being "productive"... Your concerns about what other people want you to do... Your worries about money...

Simply enjoy being with Jesus!

Rest in the Fabulous Five Virtues

You can change up this Simplifying Breath Prayer by replacing the word "rest" with each of the "Fabulous Five" virtuous states of being: faith, hope, love, joy, and peace. We see these fruitful virtues perfectly manifested in Christ our Lord.

Each of these states normally (but not always) includes pleasant, energizing emotions and yet is *larger than mere emotion.* For instance, joy and peace are often considered feelings, but really in addition to emotion they include dimensions of attitude, choice, relational connection, and bodily disposition.[100]

One at a time with each virtue try going through this breathing, simplifying prayer: "In Christ alone my soul finds faith / hope / love / joy / peace... Selah."

Soul Talk

To move from anxious overworking to joyful abiding in Christ we need the support and accountability of a good friend.

1. What is one thing you learned about Jesus' way of working?

2. Do you tend to worry or overwork? Do you feel you need to accomplish things to prove that you're adequate or to feel better in some other way? What is an example?

3. Did you practice Sabbath rest or the simplifying "In Christ Alone" prayer? If so what impact did this have on you?

Eight

No More Walking On Eggshells!

"As soon as my husband comes through the door after work I start walking on eggshells," Angelica told me. "I try so hard to make him happy, but still he gets mad at me: dinner is late, the kids didn't pick up their toys, I talk too long on the phone with my mother, or maybe he just had a bad day at the office — it's always something."

Angelica was the sweetest person you could ever meet — so friendly and pleasant to everyone, including her husband. But I knew how she felt inside. *She was angry at him* for being preoccupied with his work, having impossible expectations of her and the kids, and saying many hurtful things to her over the years.

But she was afraid to tell *him* that she was angry. "That'd just make things worse!" she insisted. She didn't want even to admit that she was mad at him because it wasn't "nice" and she hated conflict.

She couldn't bear to disappoint him and make him angry so she was tense and anxious all the time about pleasing him. Even when he was happy with her she worried because she knew that sooner or later he'd find fault with her. And then when he did criticize her she'd keep quiet and tolerate it to avoid an argument. She even clammed up when he spoke harshly with the kids, which she felt terrible about, but that's how afraid she was of his anger and how insecure she felt inside.

Of course, despite her efforts to "keep the peace," sometimes her husband did get mad at her and she'd feel hurt and abandoned. And sometimes she lost her temper (and wasn't sweet!) and then she'd blame herself and feel guilty. Whenever there was conflict she'd re-double her hyper-vigilant efforts to anticipate everything he wanted and do it for him so he wouldn't get upset. *The cycle was exhausting!*

Angelica walked on eggshells with other people too, but it was the worst with her husband. Despite the stress of carrying all that anxiety and guilt inside her, Angelica did not want to face her fear of talking to her husband about how she felt in their relationship.

"Make People Happy"

Angelica believed that she was responsible to "make" her husband and other people happy. Doing whatever she could to please people was how she showed her love. She maintained, "It's my Christian duty to do all that I can to make people happy — it'd be *selfish* not to help people and just think about what I want."

As long as she helped people, pleased them, and avoided conflict with them then she felt secure and confident. But if not then she felt anxious and guilty. She was a "mood matcher" so the only way she knew to be happy was to make her loved ones happy.

People like Angelica live by what they believe are altruistic motives like...

- "I need to make people happy."
- "I should always be nice so I don't hurt people's feelings."
- "I have to deny myself and care for other people."
- "It's selfish to think of my own needs."
- "When I see someone's problem I should always try to fix it."

Angelica believed she was offering Biblical caring to disregard herself and put all her energy into making her husband happy or fixing his problems. But it wasn't a Scriptural narrative so her life was filled with anxiety and fear. She didn't know how to walk in Jesus' easy yoke for her because she didn't have the good personal boundaries that go with his yoke.

How Are Your Boundaries?

This Boundaries Test can help you to assess if you need to strengthen your relational boundaries. Answer each question below with "yes" (mostly true for you) or "no" (mostly *not* true for you). Then circle each "yes" answer.

1. Do you tolerate mistreatment from people in hopes of being loved?

2. Do you depend on people who are emotionally unavailable to care for you?

3. Do you feel compelled to help people feel better or to solve their problems?

4. Do you rescue others from the consequences of their irresponsible behavior?

5. Do you feel empty, bored, or unimportant if you're not helping someone or responding to a crisis?

6. Is it hard for you to say "no" when someone asks you for help?

7. Is it hard for you to ask for help?

8. In close relationships do you lose interest in your own hopes and desires?

9. Are you quick to get angry about injustices done to others?

10. Do you often talk about other people and their problems?

11. Do you worry about how other people are feeling?

12. Do you worry about other people's opinions of you?

13. Do you keep quiet to avoid conflicts with people?

14. Is it hard for you to disagree with a boss or someone else in authority?

15. Do you hide things or tell "white lies" to avoid upsetting people?

16. Do you feel more comfortable giving to others rather than receiving from them?

17. Is it difficult for you to receive attention, compliments, or gifts from others?

If you have five or more yes answers, or if you answered yes to any question that is painful or problematic for you, then you probably need help developing your personal boundaries and "sense of self."

Having boundaries requires self-awareness.

Boundaries[101]

Boundaries are integral to the yoke of Jesus. So he taught us, "Simply let your 'Yes' be 'Yes,' and your 'No,' 'No'" because trying to make people to do the things you want or to think well of you "comes from the evil one" (Matthew 5:37). Jesus is telling us not to be manipulative or evasive, but to be direct and honest with people. The abilities to say yes and no and to speak the truth in love are examples of personal boundaries.

Your boundaries define your *identity.* Imagine your person like a home. You have a yard with a fence designating your property line. You have a gate at the entrance to your sidewalk and a front door to your house that locks. Inside your house is an entry way, living room, kitchen and family room, and your bedroom.

To have good boundaries begins with being *aware* of what is in each area of your property. Then you can express your *self* — the thoughts (including your beliefs and values), feelings, choices, body (including your physical needs and gifts), relationships, and soul (your longings and personality).[102] Being self-aware is always good and helpful. When you know what is important to you then you can communicate that to others and direct your actions in godly ways.

Boundaries are like a "trust door" that you open or close. Most anyone can stand at your gate outside your house, but not many people are invited all the way into your bedroom. At your home you open or close a door to someone depending upon how much you trust him or her. When you have strong boundaries you are able to say yes and let good into your personal space and you are able to say no to keep bad out.

The ability to say yes and no go together. For instance, when a difficult person wants to talk with you if you're confident in your ability to end the conversation when you need to do so (say no) then you'll be free to begin the conversation (say yes). If you're not confident you can say no then your only recourse to avoid being smothered is to duck and run!

Personal boundaries are an essential aspect of the image of God in us. God has boundaries; He is three Persons and separate from us. The Supreme Being says to us, "Be holy because I, the LORD your God, am holy" (Leviticus 19:2). Here the Almighty is proclaiming his holy identity and calling us to rely on him to help us to become holy like him.

The Bible is full of God expressing *his* identity and affirming *our* identity. He often says, "I AM" and "You are _____." (Recall the "In Christ" promises we meditated on in Chapter 5.)

Having good boundaries — self-awareness, personal responsibility, and the ability to say yes or no — is actually the basis of empathy, motivation, love, and initiative. Personal soul care, ministry to other people, capacity to do good work, and love for God are all dramatically impacted by how mature your identity-boundaries are. The stronger your sense of self, the freer you are to make choices, including to step into Jesus' easy yoke, doing all that you do with him *in* his kingdom and *for* his glory.

The Eggshells Always Break!

People like Angelica keep trying to walk on eggshells without breaking any! They tend to absorb other people's attitudes and emotions. They don't know how to be happy if their loved one is grumpy or to be at peace if their loved one is stressed. They haven't learned to maintain a separate sense of self and personal well being in the context of their relationships.

Caregivers and people in ministry are especially prone to get tied up with people who are needy, dysfunctional, abusive, addicted, or just difficult. This may be codependency.[103] Codependents have a pattern of *enmeshing* with people who have an addiction or other life problem and trying to help them. They tend to seek acceptance from unreliable or judgmental people. Inside they are afraid to be their true self and be rejected, but instead of admitting this they divert the focus to the person they're in relationship with.

As a "pleaser" Angelica focused on other people's emotions, not her own. She was always worrying about what others felt: her husband, mother, kids, friends, sister, whoever. In fact, when I asked her how she felt in her marriage invariably she answered by telling me her *perceptions* of her husband's experience:

> He's frustrated with his boss... He came home grumpy again... He doesn't like it when I cook healthy foods... He wants our kids to be more responsible, but he keeps falling behind on paying our bills... It seems like he's never happy with the kids or me... He can be real jerk...

But *unconsciously* underneath her perceptions of her husband she had painful emotions and desires that she didn't want to admit to. If she were more emotionally aware and personally responsible then she'd invite me into her heart like this:

> I'm afraid he's going to lose his job... It depresses me when he comes home stressed... I want our kids to be free to play and have fun at home and not have to worry about constantly picking up their toys... I'm angry that he doesn't help me more with the kids... I feel hurt when he doesn't like the dinner I made... I'm tired of trying so hard to please him... I feel so alone, like he doesn't really know me...

Angelica expected her husband to do for her what she was trying to do for him: *make her happy!* Her boundaries were crisscrossed — she tried to make him happy and he was supposed to make her happy! She was putting responsibility for her emotional well being on him. It was up to him to make her feel good about herself by giving her attention. It was up to him to help her feel good by coming home in a good mood. She wasn't taking responsibility for her own needs. And she was emotionally depending on someone that *she didn't feel safe with,* which reinforced her insecurity and fear.

As we explained in Chapter 2, anxiety is a symptom of trying to control people and situations and Angelica was doing a lot of that! She didn't realize it, but she was subtly *manipulating* her husband to maintain her own fragile sense of peace when she:

- Did whatever she thought her husband wanted.

- Told "white lies" if she had done something he wouldn't like.

- Was nice to her husband's face, but then talked bad about him behind his back to her mother and other people.[104]

- Nagged him and gave unsolicited advice on how he could be a better man.

- Blamed herself for making him upset.

But these behaviors just made her problems worse because she was enabling him to be irresponsible and inconsiderate and she was perpetuating her anxiety.

Which realm are you living in: the rule of God or the person you're trying to please?

Spiritually, Angelica's problem was that she wasn't living in the Kingdom of God, she was living in the kingdom of her husband. Actually, it'd be more true to say that she was living in *the kingdom of Angelica:* instead of submitting to the Lord and finding her sufficiency in him she was relying on her own abilities to make herself happy by making her husband happy.

What the Bible Actually Teaches

"Make people happy" messages are stressful narratives for life that generate a lot of pressure, guilt, and frustration. They may seem to be supported by Scripture, but careful study shows that at most they are *half-truths*. Here are five corrective Bible teachings on relationships and emotions from my seminar on "Biblical Blunders that Bruise and Confuse":[105]

1. *Sometimes love hurts.*

    Love is not always nice; it does not always make people feel good. So I often say that *there are two words for love: yes and no* (see Matthew 5:37). Jesus shows us this, as he does not always do what people want him to do. Paul gave us God's wisdom for growing up in Christ when he said, "speak the truth in love" (Ephesians 4:15). In the Gospels Jesus shows us the integration of grace and truth (John 1:14, 17).

2. *Godly self-denial comes from a loved person.*

    Jesus teaches us to deny ourselves in order to follow him in a life of love (Luke 9:23-25). But he also teaches us to love our neighbor *as we love ourselves* and to love *one another* (Mark 12:29-31; John 13:34, 15:12; see also Philippians 2:4). The psychological reality is that we cannot deny a "self" (our identity and personhood) that we haven't developed! When love is *inside* you then it can flow out of you. *God inspired self-awareness and self-esteem enables loving self-denial.*

3. *God does not want us to disregard our new self.*

    Paul also teaches us to put off our "old self" and put on our "new self" (Ephesians 4:22-24, Colossians 3:9-10). Our old self is our identity apart from Christ, self-reliant and sinful. Our new self is the "new creature" that God is making us to be as we rely on the grace of Christ (2 Corinthians 5:7). God would certainly not want us to think bad of our redeemed self!

4. There is a good "selfishness."

Jesus instructed us to ask for what we need. He put petition in the middle of the Lord's Prayer and he also told us to keep asking for what we need because God is our loving Father (Matthew 6:9-13, 7:7-11). The truth is that it's more selfish *not* to ask for what you need from people who love you because if you don't then *they'll be burdened with trying to figure out what you need and finding a way to care for you, despite your resistances.*

5. Don't do for people what they need to do for themselves.

It's not helpful to rescue people from the negative consequences of their actions — they need the pain to motivate them to change. Even in Jesus' healing ministry he gave people something to do to be made whole. So Paul taught the Galatians to help people in need without letting them be irresponsible: "Carry each other's burdens, and in this way you will fulfill the law of Christ... For each one should carry their own load" (Galatians 6:2, 5).

Adult Children and Their Mothers

For many adults the hardest person for them to have good boundaries with is their mother. And this is not because mothers are intrusive, judgmental, or controlling! Of course, some mothers, even those who are well intentioned, may have problems overriding the personal boundaries of their children. But the more typical problem in mother and adult child relationships is actually one of *closeness.*

We all need to be bonded with someone who is warm and nurturing, validates our emotions and needs, and appreciates our unique personality. And our primary source for this grace-giving, especially early in life, is our mothers. And yet our need to be attached in caring relationship is in tension with our need to be separate and to express our individuality. It may feel like meeting one need compromises the other. We may be in a stressful, confusing, push-pull of, "Come close... No, give me space."

Your needs for bonding and boundaries
are in tension with each other.

This is difficult for moms (and dad's who are closely involved). If her boundaries are not strong she may feel smothered by her child's needs for care or rejected by her child's individuation.

It's wonderful when an adult child is able to give thanks to God for their mother as David did: "You brought me out of the womb; you made me trust in you even at my mother's breast" (Psalm 22:9). Similarly, Paul's protégé Timothy experienced maternal nurture and encouragement that was central to the growth of his faith in the Lord (2 Timothy 1:5).

Of course, as we've said, sometimes even adults need personal healing and substitute mothering to get to that point of trust in the goodness of God at all times. No matter how mature we are, we all need a few people (at least one!) that we can trust and respect to mediate God's reconciling love to us (2 Corinthians 5:20).

These Christian relationships need to be *grace-giving* and *truth-revealing.* Grace provides bonding or relational connection. Truth provides boundaries or structured identity. These two primary dimensions of love manifest "the Word made flesh... who came from the Father, full of grace and truth" (John 1:14). We need to experience grace and truth in formative relationships in order to develop secure attachment with mature boundaries.

Jesus' Boundaries With His Mother

Jesus' relationship with his mother Mary is a great example of how love and boundaries belong together.

Mary demonstrates for us the posture of submission to and reliance upon God that we need in all that we do. Really, she offers the *perfect prayer* when she responds to angel's announcement that she was to participate in the immaculate conception of the Messiah and Son of God by praying: "Let it be to me according to your word" (Luke 1:38, NKJV). And she stood with John at the foot of the cross, they being the only two of Jesus' inner circle to remain faithful to him through his sufferings.

But in between these two shining examples of faith we see that Mary has some struggles in her relationship with Jesus, and he needs to set boundaries with her. As with all of our Bible heroes, we can be thankful that Mary provides us a realistic role model — we can relate to her weakness and admire her strength, relying on God's grace to progress in her Christian faith.

Even Mary had difficulty being a mom!

When Jesus was twelve years old she and Joseph took him on a spiritual pilgrimage to Jerusalem. It's hard to believe in our society today, but this was a rite of passage into spiritual *adulthood* for Jesus. And when he was in Jerusalem he went off on his own to go the temple and there he interacted with the religious leaders in deep conversation about the Holy Scriptures and he astounded them all with his wisdom.

Mary did not know where Jesus was and after a few days she understandably became quite worried and upset. When she finally found Jesus she blurted out: "Young man! Why have you treated us like this? Your father and I have been worried sick looking all over Jerusalem trying to find you!" (Luke 2:48, paraphrased).

Jesus responded: "Why were you so anxious and searching for me? You should have known that I'd be in my Father's house doing his work" (Luke 2:49, paraphrased). Notice that Jesus does not take responsibility for his mother being upset with him — he doesn't feel bad or guilty. Nor does he react with anger at her apparent guilt trip. In fact, we read: "Then Jesus went down to Nazareth with them and was obedient to them" (Luke 2:51).

Jesus developed strong personal boundaries.

Imagine being suddenly scolded from your mother in the midst of an intense discussion on your job or in a family situation. How did twelve year old Jesus remain so calm, so secure, so loving? Where did he get the presence of mind to speak the truth in love so clearly and respectfully in the midst of a very stressful situation?

The answer to Jesus' strength goes back to our theme song: *Jesus was in the easy yoke! He was standing in the invisible kingdom of his Father who loved him!* Even as a young man he was able to maintain a *separate emotional grounding* from Mary's frustration (also the religious leaders' opinions of him) because he was in a "unique Father-Son operation, coming out of Father and Son intimacies and knowledge."

Jesus demonstrated the same healthy boundaries years later when he was beginning his public ministry. He was at the Cana wedding with Mary and she seems to put pressure on him to fix her friends' problem of having run out of wine. He calmly and matter of factly set a limit with her and told her that this was not his problem. But then in secret he went ahead and miraculously changed the water into wine to bless the host and wedding party and, more importantly, to reveal his glory to his disciples (John 2:1-11).

Then not long after this when Jesus was ministering in a house that was jam-packed and overflowing with people his boundaries were again tested. His mother and brothers heard about the situation and "they went to take charge of him, for they said, 'He is out of his mind.'" Perhaps they wanted to take Jesus back to Nazareth to their family home and carpenter's shop.

But again Jesus did not let Mary's (or his siblings') desires *define or control him*. He spoke the truth in love and said no; he insisted that he was going to stay in the house and continue teaching the people and healing those who were sick. In fact, they should join him in doing God's will! (Mark 3:20-21, 31-35).

Jesus Set Boundaries in His Helping

The way Jesus was with Mary is the way he was with everyone. He never walked on eggshells around people, worrying about upsetting them, clinging to them for approval, or pushing to get them to do what they should. He was self-aware, secure, solid, purposeful, straightforward, loving. The Gospels are full of examples of our Master's clear and assertive identity:[106]

- Jesus accepted the limits of 24 hours in a day, being in one place at a time, and having just three years of public ministry.

- He set boundaries on inappropriate behavior.

- He disagreed with the Pharisees and other authority figures.

- He spoke the truth in love.

- He walked away from entire villages of needy people when the Father said it was time to go to another place.

- Our Savior who came to be crucified walked away from murderous crowds ready to stone him or throw him off a cliff.

- He walked away from applauding crowds that wanted to make him a political king or miracle worker on demand.

- He withdrew from people to pray by the lake or in the hills.

- He said yes to some friends and no to others, taking only Peter, James, and John on retreat with him.

- He said no to his ambitious disciples.

- He expected everyone he helped to *act with faith* in order to be healed or to make a life change.

The Tekton-Rabbi's wise boundaries gave him the power to love well. For instance, he loved his enemies in ways that left an indelible imprint with people and inspired them to believe in him. He even taught natural enemies to love each other. He took Simon the Zealot who hated Roman oppression and Matthew the tax collector who served Rome and brought them into his company of Twelve and they learned to accept one another and to serve Christ together.

Say no to lesser things in order
to say yes to what is *best.*

The Psalm 1 Man

Psalm 1 gives us a great picture of a man with strong personal boundaries who *lives vibrantly in the Divine Dominion.* He rejects worldly counsel and sinful ways to delight in and meditate on the law of God — the Word or message of God's loving purposes — day and night. "He is like a tree planted by streams of water, which yields its fruit in season and whose leaf does not wither. Whatever he does prospers" (v. 3).

As a Psalm 1 person, even under the pressure of sweltering heat and drought your leaves stay green and you have the capacity to bear fruit because your roots go down deep to drink in the stream of life. Even when people are offensive you don't internalize it to become wounded or ashamed by it, you don't react in anger, but remain separate and secure in your personal boundaries, rooted in God's kingdom of light. You're defined not by the visible landscape of conflict, but by the *invisible landscape* of the Father's glorious spiritual world. Therefore you're able to bear the fruit of love to someone who is hurtful or even downright mean. You can offer undeserved forgiveness or respond to criticism with empathy and kindness.

This is a picture of the clear and strong boundaries that go with becoming more like Jesus Christ, *the perfect Psalm 1 Man.*

How Angelica Simplified Her Life

Angelica took ownership of her emotions and took courage to verbalize her feelings and desires to her husband. She asked him when she needed help with the kids or for the two of them to talk without interruption. She spoke the truth in love by telling him she felt hurt when he didn't show appreciation for dinner. She told him when she felt the kids needed new clothes.

Also she stopped agreeing with him too quickly. For instance, his mother wanted to stay in their home for two weeks and she said, "Let me pray about that and get back to you." She was separating herself from on the spot pressure to please him and buying time to get perspective. This helped her decide to set a limit of a one week stay.

Another example of Angelica setting a boundary was in her house cleaning. Previously she accepted her husband's pressure to keep the house immaculate. Instead of kowtowing to his demands she kept the house clean, but didn't stress about keeping it perfect. She stopped *enabling* his bad behavior.

Instead of being yoked to her husband's perfectionism she learned to be yoked to Jesus' mercy.

Experiment

Boundaries

We need to practice disciplines for the spiritual life because it's only by applying God's wisdom to our particular life situations that we learn and grow. We don't become more like Jesus merely by reading or studying (as important as these disciplines are), but by holding Christ's hand as we step out into the unknown, trying something new with our gracious Lord.

Joshua says to us, "Choose for yourselves this day whom you will serve... But as for me and my household, we will serve the LORD" (Joshua 24:15). Your opportunity this week is to choose to serve the Lord by setting boundaries in a relationship that is dysfunctional or is causing undo stress. To say no simplifies your life and frees up more space and energy so that you can be more devoted to the Lord and serving him.

To express personal limitations that may be unpopular with some people requires that you *trust the sufficiency of God for yourself and for others.* The Psalmist prays,

God is my refuge and strength, an ever-present help in trouble... You are my portion, O LORD... You are a shield all around me, O LORD; you bestow glory on me and lift up my head... [You] brought me out into a spacious place... The boundary lines have fallen in pleasant places for me (Psalm 46:1, 119:57, 3:3, 18:19, 16:6).

The Psalmist is inviting us to follow his example of learning to be secure and happy in the spiritual presence of the Lord God as our Eternal Refuge, even as we're dealing with conflict or mistreatment. We don't have to accommodate to whatever people want, try to impress them, or carry the weight of their problems — *we can remain rooted in God's great grace.*

No matter how bad our circumstances are
we're safe if we're in God's eternal kingdom.

Setting boundaries is more than a psychological tool — it's really a spiritual discipline that helps to establish further your self-identity in Christ and your place in his Spacious Land of Light and Love. By saying no to straining to make people happy or rescue them we can *yes to Christ's rule in our lives and theirs.* The reverse is also true: Saying yes to Christ in new and deeper ways gives us added strength to say no, even if it might escalate tensions or disappoint someone.

Oftentimes, to set a boundary requires that you let go of a way that you have felt (or tried to feel) in control of things through seeking approval from people, being nice and sweet, getting something done "right," or being helpful. If you're used to doing these things then relinquishing your perceived control will probably increase your anxiety at first. But it's only by facing our fears that we can overcome them.

By living within your personal limitations you can venture on God to see what he'll do when you make space for him to act in your life and in the relationship you're concerned about. You're venturing on God to see if over time you don't discover that it's really true: Jesus' yoke is easy — *including for the person(s) you're having difficulty with!* Trusting God's sufficiency for others helps you to say no or speak the truth when needed.

Live with Christ as your Center

The power and peace of the easy yoke is that just as Jesus lived Father-centered so we can learn to live Jesus-centered. It's a priority; it's a boundary that's up to us to understand, define, and live out in the context of our daily life and relationships.

Good boundaries are central to Jesus' message to us in Matthew 11. "The is a unique Father-Son operation," he says. "No one knows the Son the way the Father does, nor the Father the way the Son does." Two persons with separate identities have chosen to be one, with the Holy Spirit, while maintaining and celebrating one another's uniqueness. The members of the Godhead know each other intimately and partner together, in the works of creation, redemption, and Kingdom living for all creatures. This is their priority and they continually set limits along these lines. Christ is showing us exactly what the Trinitarian life looks like in a human being.

Thomas Kelly, a Quaker missionary and teacher of the early 20th Century, wrote about the importance of developing great boundaries in order to become "skilled in the inner life" and pull out "the real roots of our problem."[107] He impassions us to simplify our lives so that we function from "a divine Center."[108]

The outer distractions of our interests reflect an inner lack of integration of our own lives. We are trying to be several selves at once, without all our selves being organized by a single, mastering Life within us. Each of us tends to be, not a single self, but a whole committee of selves... It is as if we have a chairman of our committee of the many selves within us, who does not integrate the many into one but who merely counts the votes at each decision...

We have seen and known some people who seem to have found this deep Center of living, where the fretful calls of life are integrated, where No as well as Yes can be said with confidence. We've seen such lives, integrated, unworried by the tangles of close decisions, unhurried, cheery, fresh, and positive. These are not people of dallying idleness nor of obviously mooning meditation; they are busy carrying their full load as well as we, but without any chafing of the shoulders with the burden, with quiet joy and springing step. Surrounding the trifles of their daily life is an aura of infinite peace and power and joy...

Let me talk very intimately and very earnestly with you about Him who is dearer than life. Do you really want to live your lives, every moment of your lives, in His Presence? Do you long for Him, crave Him? Do you love His Presence? Does every drop of blood in your body love Him? Does every breath you draw breathe a prayer, a praise to Him? Do you sing and dance within yourselves, as you glory in His love? Have you set yourselves to be His, and *only* His, walking every moment in holy obedience?

If you say you haven't the time to go down into the recreating silences, I can only say to you, 'Then you don't *really* want to, you don't yet love God above all else in the world, with all your heart and soul and mind and strength.' ...We find time for what we *really want* to do.[109]

Four Ways to Start Setting Boundaries

Here are some practical ideas for how you can strengthen your boundary muscles by setting your limits and centering down in Christ:

1. Don't deny your emotions.

Have you been repressing feelings of being hurt or pressured by someone? Or have you been hiding things to avoid conflict? Instead of internalizing stress to keep peace tell your friend or family member how you feel (emotions themselves are not sinful), while being careful not to be critical or blaming. Take the posture that you are simply *inviting this person to understand your emotions and needs.*

2. Don't depend on unsafe people.

Are you emotionally depending on a person for approval who is not a safe Christ's Ambassador for you? Instead, bring your personal needs to people you trust and respect.

3. Don't be the hero!

Do you feel pressure to be super-responsible about something when there is someone else who could also be involved to help? Wait before you jump in to be the hero — trust Jesus Christ to be the Savior! Give someone else a chance to be used by God.

4. Don't be sucked dry.

Are you *always* saying yes to needy people? Sometimes you need to say no or limit the time you give. Use the freed up time to connect with God in quiet or to be with someone that renews your soul. Being replenished and strengthening your boundary muscles will help you to be a cheerful giver.

A Breath Prayer From the Bible

You may feel anxious about the prospect of saying no to someone or having a difficult conversation, but don't let that stop you! *Try it from within the blessed yoke of Jesus.*

To help you "take courage" from Christ I invite you to meditate on Paul's words in Philippians 4. He wrote these powerful, Spirit-inspired words when he was being persecuted in jail. (For him being in jail meant being chained to a prison guard who probably was a boring, smelly, foul-mouthed, brute thug!)

> Rejoice in the Lord always. I will say it again: Rejoice!... Do not be anxious about anything... If anything is excellent or praiseworthy — think about such things...

> I have learned to be content whatever the circumstances. I know what it is to be in need, and I know what it is to have plenty. I have learned the secret of being content in any and every situation, whether well fed or hungry, whether living in plenty or in want. I can do everything through him who gives me strength (Philippians 4:4, 6, 8, 11-13).

Paul wasn't defined by his visible circumstance of being chained to an ogre — *he was appreciating that he was in the wide-open spaces of the Trinitarian Society!* The peace of Christ was "guarding" his mind and heart (v 7). Nourished by his life within the boundaries of God's wonderful kingdom, he wasn't anxious, resentful, or complaining about the injustice of his situation — he was quite happy within the boundaries of Jesus' easy yoke!

Being yoked within the boundaries of God's kingdom frees us from anxiety and agitation.

I invite you to cultivate Paul's reliance upon God's wonderful empire in our midst. The Lord's spiritual fortress is a place of strong boundaries that can help you to find peace as you *de-enmesh yourself* from stress-filled relationships.

We need to learn to let go of trying to control our relationships and accept that they may be harmonious or they may be conflictual, but either way I can trust the Sovereign Lord's loving rule in my life. I abandon outcomes to God because I trust that he is working all things together for my good (Romans 8:28). This helps us to be more loving toward difficult people.

To build up your separate boundaries in relationship to others you can try my Breath Prayer adapted from Philippians 4:11-13: "In Christ I'm strong... in conflict or harmony." It's a simple way to pray the peace of our Father's eternal world deep into our hearts, letting it, rather than our stress, shape and form us.

It's helpful to use this Breath Prayer to watch and pray with Jesus by *anticipating* a conflict, guilt trip, or other stress on your boundaries in a particular relationship. Imagine yourself in the stressful relationship situation... Talk to your gracious Lord and Savior about how you feel... Now offer the Breath Prayer:

- Breathe in to receive the Lord's blessing: "In Christ I'm strong..."

- Breathe out to let go, trusting the outcomes to the Sovereign Lord: "In conflict or harmony."

- Inhale (trust) the reality of the heavens all around you: "In Christ I'm strong..."

- Exhale to refuse to be defined by your visible circumstances: "In conflict or harmony."

You may find it better fits your particular need to alter the wording to one of these prayers:

- "In Christ I'm strong... To help others or to set a limit."
- "In Christ I'm strong... When mistreated or loved."
- "In Christ I'm strong... When praised or criticized."
- "In Christ I'm strong... When alone or accepted."

Or, still staying with Paul's teaching in Philippians 4, you can substitute the word "content" for strong: "In Christ I'm *content...* in conflict or harmony."

Soul Talk

Support from friends who give us empathy is what gives us the strength to set limits and refuse to walk on eggshells.

1. What are you learning about life in God's kingdom and setting boundaries in your relationships?

2. Do you enmesh with other people emotionally or do too much to help them? What is an example?

3. How did you do with setting boundaries this week and finding security and strength in Jesus' easy yoke?

Nine

God's Wildflower
(Help for Perfectionism)

A youth pastor named Justin was overstressed. He was doing a great job with his high school students, but he didn't feel like it because he kept comparing himself to other pastors who he thought were more successful than him.

Whenever a student wasn't paying attention to his message or stopped attending meetings he took it personally. He thought to himself, *I'm not as dynamic as other youth pastors. I need to make things more exciting so more students will come.*

I asked Justin, "Who is saying you need to be a better youth pastor?"

"The Senior Pastor," he replied. "He's putting pressure on me to get more kids involved. And he's right our numbers are down."

"How about when you were growing up? Did anyone talk to you in that tone?"

"Well, I was never able to be good enough for my father, but we didn't have much of a relationship. He divorced my mom when I was in high school and moved to another state. Even before then he wasn't around much and when he was home he was drinking.

"I remember when I was about seven or eight years old I kept asking him to play catch with me and finally one day we did. He actually bought me a glove and a ball — I was so excited! But I was having trouble learning to throw. He tried to teach me, but he got frustrated with me and I started crying. I did my best when I threw him the ball, but I was awkward and my throws were bad. Finally he yelled, 'Justin, you throw like a girl! Why can't you be like your older brother?' and he walked away.

"That's what it was like. My grades weren't good enough because I didn't get A's like my little sister. And I didn't play sports or do anything as good as my brother."

All Justin wanted was his dad's approval. But he had almost no connection with him, except to hear about what he was doing wrong. He knew his father was wrong to be that way. Justin had forgiven him, but on a deeper level he couldn't get free of feeling like he had to excel in order to be acceptable. He felt like an "average pastor" and that felt bad. Until he was a *standout* pastor who was recognized for having a great ministry he couldn't relax.

"Make Yourself Stand Out"

I relate to Justin's anxious struggle to do better. Probably sometimes you also feel like you're not _____ enough. Not pretty enough. Not smart enough. Not wealthy enough. Not popular enough. Not accomplishing enough. Not holy enough.

Early in the nearly two decade long period that I was fasting from publishing books Kristi and I were on a retreat with a group of Christian leaders. We were getting away for some days of teaching, community, and solitude. We practiced a variety of spiritual disciplines together and separately, all designed to help us to connect more intimately with Jesus so that we could become more like him in life and ministry.

Being quiet and still before God opened up my heart so I became aware of feeling deficient. I felt I was not doing enough with my life: I was not excelling in Christian ministry like some of my peers. They were writing books and leading seminars and retreats and being commended. They were living out my dreams!

When we believe the lie that we are "not enough" we're being choked by an un-Christly, anxious yoke. Our soul can't breathe the air of heaven when we're driven into shame or envy. Worried about our performance and ourselves, we're not prepared to give the people we interact with the blessing from God that they need.

Christians are not exempt from trying to stand out! Probably you're familiar with some of these common motivational sayings:

- "Give your all to do better."
- "You never get a second chance to make a first impression."
- "Strive to be better than your competition."
- "Develop the will to win."
- "Climb to the top of the ladder."
- "You're only as good as your last performance."

Are these messages good coaching? As you deal with challenges in your business, relationships, or ministry is God urging you to make yourself stand out? Is this the way to overcome feeling inadequate and insecure?

Are You a Perfectionist?

Many people I talk to have been formed by a "make yourself stand out" narrative. This leads to the perfectionism of anxiously relying on your own abilities to be more ideal in some way. Here's a short test to help you see if you have perfectionistic tendencies. For each question below answer "yes" if it's generally true of you and "no" if it's generally *not* true of you.

1. I often think that I should've done better than I did.
2. I tend to put things off if I don't have the time to do them perfectly.
3. I'm afraid to fail when working on an important project.
4. I strive to impress others with my best qualities or accomplishments.
5. I think less of myself if I repeat a mistake.
6. I strive to maintain control of my emotions at all times.
7. I get upset when things don't go as planned.
8. I am often disappointed in the quality of other people's work.

9. I feel that my standards should always be real high.

10. I'm afraid that people will think less of me if I fail.

11. I'm constantly trying to improve myself.

12. I'm unhappy if anything I do is considered average.

13. My home and office need to be clean and orderly always.

14. I feel inferior to others who are more intelligent, attractive, or successful than I am.

15. I must look my very best whenever I'm out in public.

If you have five or more yes answers to these questions it suggests that you struggle with perfectionism and need to absorb more of God's grace.

The Grace Antidote

The "You can do better! Make yourself stand out!" message is common today in Christian coaching, counseling, motivational talks, self-help books, and sermons. It helps some people achieve outward success, but it's opposed to Jesus' Gospel.

Besides, trying to be ideal doesn't work! It's a never-ending performance treadmill. No matter how good you look or how much you achieve or how much recognition and attention you get it won't be enough, it won't fill your soul's tummy. Nobody knows the real you and so you're left *empty of grace.* You're left feeling insecure and inadequate, if not ashamed and worthless.

When I became envious of my friends that day on retreat I was being assaulted by this faulty, self-aggrandizing thinking. The world, my flesh (natural abilities apart from God), and the devil were ganging up on me to take me out of the mind of Christ (including the truths of Scripture that took on flesh and blood in Jesus Christ). Without realizing it, *I was turning away from Christ's smile and his open arms to me and turning to myself to get what I wanted.* I was believing some of Satan's lies and half-truths that buzz around in our airwaves.

To us who strive to succeed or to win people's approval Jesus offers his counter-cultural Easy Yoke Gospel. He looks right at you, smiles, and says, "Are you tired? Are you worn out?... Come to me. Get away with me and you'll recover your life... Walk with me... Learn the unforced rhythms of grace... I won't lay anything heavy or ill-fitting on you. Keep company with me and you'll learn to live freely and lightly."

Jesus welcomes you! Lay your burden down. You don't have to be ideal. You don't have to do everything right. You don't have to please everybody. You are loved and accepted for who you are!

You're not not a human *doing* — you're a human *being,* loved by God.

Jesus Resisted Competitiveness

Before the Son of the Highest came on the public scene John the Baptist was recognized as the greatest prophet by all the people of Israel. People from all over Israel and beyond — men and women, the rich and the poor, the religious and the uneducated — journeyed into the desert to find John the Baptist and he would teach them to turn from their sins to Yahweh and then he'd baptize them in the Jordan River to symbolize that God was cleansing their sin and giving them a fresh start.

Probably the high point of John's ministry was when Jesus, the long-awaited Christ and John's own cousin, came to *him* to be baptized, even though he had no sin to wash away. The Baptist was the forerunner leading up to the Messiah and the one who was chosen by God to help him launch his public ministry!

But from that point forward Jesus' ministry grew and John's declined. John's best disciples left him to follow Jesus. Fewer and fewer people went to John to be baptized and more and more went to Jesus' followers. And people noticed this. In fact, they started keeping score and told John he was losing!

But John did not react with jealousy or competitive ambition — he didn't want to make himself stand out, *he wanted to make Christ stand out!* He said Jesus was the Bridegroom, the people of God were his bride, and John himself was only the friend of the Bridegroom. He said that his joy was to attend to the Bridegroom's needs and bless his relationship with his bride (John 3:29).

He summarized his life purpose in perhaps the most humble and God-glorifying words of the whole Bible: "[Jesus] must become greater; I must become less" (John 3:30).

Pray, "More of Jesus... Less of me..."

Let's turn to Jesus' part in the story. Look at his reaction to people making a contest between the number of baptisms performed by him versus by John. "When the Lord learned of this, he left Judea and went back once more to Galilee" (John 4:3).

Jesus did not give into temptations to jealousy or competitiveness toward John the Baptist or anyone. In fact, our Savior didn't even want to draw attention to his successes! When he performed miracles he often asked people to keep it secret.[110] When his popularity surged with the crowds he withdrew. When people praised him he put the spotlight on the Father. In everything he sought to glorify the Father's name.

Jesus Became a Seed for Us

In the Gospel of John we find that Jesus seems to resist the temptation to compete as a great public speaker (John 12:20-26). Some God-fearing Greek men had came to Jerusalem to worship at the Passover Feast. They had heard about Jesus' great wisdom and miracles and used the Apostle Philip, who had a Greek name and probably spoke Greek, to get an interview with Jesus.

The Greeks were known in that day for their profound philosophies about life and religion. Apparently they wanted Jesus to come share his ideas with their people in the great cities of the Roman world like Rome, Alexandria, and Antioch. What an opportunity for Jesus to advance his career as a public speaker and take his brilliance to the world! He could show that his ideas for life were far superior to that of Plato and Aristotle!

The Jews wanted Jesus to be their long-awaited Messiah-king to overthrow the Roman government and return the state of Israel to the glory years of David (John 6:15). Indeed Jesus had the the ability to rule the world like the greatest Caesar ever. One way he could gain more popularity and power, elevating himself and zionist Israel with him, was to expand his influence among the Greeks. Some of the Jews were talking about this (John 7:35).

No doubt Jesus' ambitious apostles would've been happy to accompany him on a tour through the Roman world and to watch him humble the Greek philosophers as he'd done repeatedly with the Jewish religion scholars. They could ride on the coattails of their brilliant teacher's expanding career!

Jesus' answer to his ambitious followers was to tell a story:

There was a kernel of wheat that was clinging to its stalk. And it decided to stop clutching onto the life it knew and fall off the stalk to the ground. It let go of life on its own terms and was buried in the earth. Then the rains came and the sun shined and a little seedling came up. In time it grew to be a wheat plant with lots of new seeds.

The seed had died. It gave up its life when it let go of the stalk. It disappeared. If you went to the spot where the seed fell and looked for it on the ground or under the surface of the ground you wouldn't find it. It was gone. The kernel of wheat gave up its life to produce new life.[111]

In effect Jesus was saying:

I am that seed that dies. I've let go of this world. I'm not clinging to my rights and my privileges and my opportunities. I'm not going to advance my career as a speaker. I'm not using my power to establish Israel as the world superpower. I've denied myself these things. I even let go of the privileges of my position in the Trinity in heaven and I took on human flesh to come to earth.

Instead of trying to make things happen for myself, I've submitted to the Father and given him charge of my life. So he has given me *his* life and he is producing from my life, many, many new seeds of abundant and eternal life.

Now I'm about to go to the cross to be crucified. I'm doing this to save you from your sins and to show you unequivocally how to let go of trying to control your life and instead give it away to God. Then you can join me and participate in divine, ever-lasting living!

Jesus chose the cross rather than advancing his public speaking career in Greece.

Paul Shows Us How to Be Like Jesus

Paul shows us how to be as a seed that lets go of its stalk and falls to the ground and dies to produce many more seeds for God's glory. According to tradition he was a short man. In fact, Paul means "small." Maybe he tried to compensate and this is why he was so ambitious and proud of his superlative pedigree and list of achievements. He was perhaps the greatest and most accomplished Pharisee of his day. He was "top dog" in the religious world, which in that culture meant he received the highest respect. But after he saw the Light of Christ on the Damascus Road he brought all of his ambition to the cross.

Paul had been a wild stallion and he learned that he needed the Lord to corral and tame his cutthroat nature. So he took off his religious image and he discarded it like a cloak. He went off into the Arabian Desert in solitude and silence and with the risen Christ, apparently for three years (Galatians 1:15-18).

He was taught by the Spirit of Jesus and came into a profound and passionate love for his Lord. He urges us to join him and take our competitiveness and jealousy to the cross:

> If you have any encouragement from being united with Christ, if any comfort from his love, if any fellowship with the Spirit, if any tenderness and compassion, then make my joy complete by being like-minded, having the same love, being one in spirit and purpose. Do nothing out of selfish ambition or vain conceit, but in humility consider others better than yourselves. Each of you should look not only to your own interests, but also to the interests of others (Philippians 2:1-4).

Then, quoting a hymn from the first days of the Church, he teaches us to make our attitude the same as that of Christ Jesus who left heaven and "made himself nothing" as a human servant (Philippians 2:7).

As Christ emptied himself of personal privileges and prosperities for the Father so Paul emptied himself for Christ:

> But whatever was to my profit I now consider loss for the sake of Christ. What is more, I consider everything a loss compared to the surpassing greatness of knowing Christ Jesus my Lord, for whose sake I have lost all things. I consider them rubbish, that I may gain Christ and be found in him, not having a righteousness of my own that comes from the law, but that which is through faith in Christ — the righteousness that comes from God and is by faith. I want to know Christ and the power of his resurrection and the fellowship of sharing in his sufferings, becoming like him in his death, and so, somehow, to attain to the resurrection from the dead (Philippians 3:7-11).

The Alpha Dog apostle became the humblest, most generous, most Christlike apprentice! What a helpful role model Paul is. Like us, he didn't have the advantage of physically being with Jesus for three years as the other apostles. He learned to relate with the risen Christ, invisible to the physical eye and present only to the eye of faith. Through the testimony of the Gospel writers and other Apostles, his years of quiet prayer in the desert, and practicing other disciplines for a spiritual life in Christ, he learned to live with *passionate indifference:* he cultivated an intense attachment to Christ and detached from everything else!

Be passionately indifferent to all things except knowing Christ with others!

A Wildflower in a Field of Flowers

Jesus' Easy Yoke Message begins with Matthew commenting, "Abruptly Jesus broke into prayer." It's a hinge point. The Master shifts from denouncing stubborn cities behind him to "tenderly" caring for the weary folk at hand. Then he prays out loud, "Thank you, Father, Lord of heaven and earth. You've concealed your ways from sophisticates and know-it-alls, but spelled them out clearly to ordinary people. Yes, Father, that's the way you like to work."

Ordinary people. Not the extraordinary. Not those garnering success and power in religion or culture. The people that nobody notices — *except God.*

In my family of origin I was a Hero Child. I scored touchdowns. I got A's. I memorized the most Bible verses. I was a good boy. Eventually I burned out.

But in my spiritual renewal I discovered that *it's a gift to be an ordinary person in the Father's world!* I appreciated this one spring day in 2005 when I was walking and pouring out my heart to Jesus about feeling inadequate. He began showing me what a glorious scene he had created for me to be in with him: the sun was shining on us, the birds were singing over us, and we were walking along a path that cut through a valley filled with wildflowers.

I felt impressed to stop and *really look* at all the wildflowers in front of me. There were so many! They were so colorful! And they were just there because God wanted them there. No person had planted them. God sent breezes and birds to scatter seeds and he sent rain and sun and grew the flowers. Thousands of people drove by this valley every day just a block or two from where I was standing and yet very few of them ever walked over to appreciate these flowers.

Then God showed me a *single wildflower* surrounded by thousands of other flowers. I sensed him whisper to my heart:

Be like that flower before me. See how beautiful it is? See how happy it is? And yet it is lost in a sea of color and fragrance.

No one has ever laid eyes on that flower alone — those who stand where you are might see the whole field of wildflowers, but not this particular one. You say, "This flower does not stand out — it's not special." But *I appreciate this flower!* It is beautiful to me! And it is joining with all the other flowers in this valley to communicate my goodness and love to passersby.

I often thank God for that wildflower! I remind myself to bloom where I am planted for God — even if no one else seems to notice. I'm a wildflower in the Father's field of flowers and *so are you!* He's planted us, given us beauty and sweet fragrance, and we're blossoming, not individually, but together in community for *Him,* the angels, and the people around us.

The Wildflower in the Bible

Later I noticed the same wildflower in a field when praying Psalm 103. *I Am God's Flower* is my paraphrase of verses 15-17:

As for me, my days are like grass,
I flourish like a wildflower in the Father's field,
Given life and color by the Son;
The Spirit blows over me and I am gone to heaven,
And my place remembers me no more.
But from everlasting to everlasting
The Lord's love is with me, as I revere him,
And his righteousness is with my children's children.

Probably David's words inspired Jesus when he said: "See how the lilies of the field grow? Your Father clothes them in splendor. So much more than this he clothes you and loves you!" (Matthew 6:28-30, paraphrase). The Psalmist and the Savior helped me to write *God's Wildflower:*

My precious wildflower — smile!
I have clothed you in heaven's splendor.
Though you're lost to all in a field of blooms,
You're seen by me and my sweet society.
Don't worry about who sees your beauty
Or about how much time you have to bloom.
Be dead to the world and alive to me
For I planted you here and I know your name.

I am your Father smiling over you!
You're growing in the grace of my Sonlight,
Nourished by the rains from my mouth.
My choirs of angels, birds, and saints
Join me in singing my love song over you;
We delight to dance with you in Spirit breezes.
What joy it brings to us all in my kingdom
When you smile and sing back to me!

God's words are always blossoming if only we will stop, look, and smell their fragrance! The Holy Spirit ministers the living word of God — the Word of the Bible (2 Timothy 3:16), the divine voice that is continually speaking in thoughts and impressions (Psalm 19:1-4; 1 John 2:20, 27), the word of the Gospel (Mark 4:14), the Word made flesh in Jesus Christ (John 1:14)[112] — so that "in [God] we live and move and have our being" (Acts 17:28).

God creates and sustains all life through his words (Psalm 19, Hebrews 4:12, 1 Peter 1:23). God's communications (which are always in tune with the Bible if they're genuine) are not only true, they're real — they're *reality*. God's voice to us is like the manna that fell from heaven in the desert wilderness and the Israelites ate it and lived off of it for forty years (Exodus 16:4, Psalm 78:24). In this way, God's message to me that I am his little flower in a field of flowers has nourished me and many others.

Let's ask, "Am I drawing attention to myself or to Jesus?"

The Lord has Especially Chosen *You!*

Jeanne Guyon (1648-1717) was a French mystic who was persecuted by the religious authorities of the Catholic Church for her writings that empowered simple people to go directly to God through praying the Scriptures from their hearts. Let's *take heart* from her! She has helped countless ordinary people live in the Father's field as glorious wildflowers![113]

I give you an invitation: If you are thirsty, come to the living waters. Do not waste your precious time digging wells that have no water in them. If you are starving and can find nothing to satisfy your hunger, then come. Come, and you will be filled.

You who are poor, come.

You who are afflicted, come...

Dear child of God, your Father has His arms of love open wide to you. Throw yourself into His arms. You who have strayed and wandered away as sheep, return to your Shepherd...

I especially address those of you who are very simple and you who are uneducated... You may think yourself the one farthest from a deep experience with the Lord; but, in fact, the Lord has *especially* chosen you! You are the one *most* suited to know Him well...

So let no one feel left out. Jesus Christ has called us all.

Oh, I suppose there is one group who *is* left out!

Do not come if you have no heart. You see, before you come, there is one thing you must do: You must first give your heart to the Lord...

Once you have enjoyed your Lord and tasted the sweetness of His love [through praying the Scriptures and beholding Christ], you will find that even your selfish desires no longer hold any power. You will find it impossible to have pleasure in anything except Him...

I realize that some of you may feel that you are very slow, that you have a poor understanding, and that you are very unspiritual. Dear reader, there is nothing in this universe that is easier to obtain than the enjoyment of Jesus Christ! Your Lord is more present to you than you are to yourself! Furthermore, His desire to give Himself to you is *greater* than *your* desire to lay hold of Him.[114]

The enjoyment of Christ is the easiest thing in the universe to experience!

God is saying the same thing to us through Jeanne Guyon as the little wildflower: "You are significant to me! You are beautiful to me! Just be who I made you to be and let me love you. Stand tall and smile where I've placed you. Don't worry about who notices you. Just let your light shine for me."

This is the message of God's grace that helped Justin begin to experience healing from his anxious perfectionism. He had to trust his heavenly Father at a deeper level and let go of his earthly father's rejections. Previously, he "knew" that the message of God's grace was throughout the Bible — he preached sermons on it! — but he didn't *know* it deep in his heart. But now he was learning how to rely on God's *unconditional love* in the context of his daily life and church work. He was discovering how to rest in Jesus' easy yoke of peace.

Experiment

Blessing Your Competitors

Jesus' teaching that we love people who mistreat us is the highpoint of his ethic, which stands far above that of all competing religions:

To you who are ready for the truth, I say this: Love your enemies. Let them bring out the best in you, not the worst. When someone gives you a hard time, respond with the energies of prayer for that person. If someone slaps you in the face, stand there and take it. If someone grabs your shirt, giftwrap your best coat and make a present of it. If someone takes unfair advantage of you, use the occasion to practice the servant life. No more tit-for-tat stuff. Live generously.

Here is a simple rule of thumb for behavior: Ask yourself what you want people to do for you; then grab the initiative and do it for *them*! If you only love the lovable, do you expect a pat on the back? Run-of-the-mill sinners do that. If you only help those who help you, do you expect a medal? Garden-variety sinners do that. If you only give for what you hope to get out of it, do you think that's charity? The stingiest of pawnbrokers does that.

I tell you, love your enemies. Help and give without expecting a return. You'll never — I promise — regret it. Live out this God-created identity the way our Father lives toward us, generously and graciously, even when we're at our worst. Our Father is kind; you be kind (Luke 6:27-36, MSG).

These words on agape for enemies aren't just the words of a rabbi, they're also the words of a tekton. Most of all, they are the words of *the Lamb of God who died on a cross for the sins of the world.*

Paul followed Jesus' way of radical love when he was wrongly criticized, beaten, imprisoned, and stoned: "When we are cursed, we bless; when we are persecuted, we endure it; when we are slandered, we answer kindly" (1 Corinthians 4:12-13). He urged us also to follow Jesus' way: "Bless those who persecute you; bless and do not curse." (Romans 12:14).

But it's Hard to Love Enemies!

In our apprentice to Christ training we pray, "Today, I look to love others as you love me, dear God, blessing everyone I meet, even those who mistreat me."

But how many Christians can consistently and joyfully love people who say or do hurtful things to them? Is it even a genuine goal of ours? Have you ever been to a seminar or even heard a sermon on *learning how* to bless those who curse you?[115]

Many people I talk with, pastors among them, simply are not able to give the gentle answer that turns away anger (Proverbs 15:1). Instead they react with insecure defensiveness, more anger, or become withdrawn and depressed. Some vulnerable Christians, trying to obey the Lord, fall into patterns of continually being abused and feeling fear and shame when they're mistreated.

To bless those that curse you is not being

a doormat — it's being a *doorway to heaven.*

Recall our earlier discussion about bonding and boundaries. The Lord doesn't want you to be mistreated in ways that leave you feeling bad about yourself or frightened of more mistreatment! But neither does he want you following worldly ways of selfishness and fighting. Instead, he wants to heal our emotional wounds, strengthen our weaknesses, and grow our immaturity so that we develop the strength of character to be able to be kind to those who are mean to us and do it with strong internal boundaries and a healthy sense of our belovedness and value.

Dallas Willard teaches that to learn how to love our enemies we can begin by blessing our *competitors,* which is a smaller challenge and one that comes up frequently in our relationships with loved ones, friends, neighbors, and co-workers.[116]

Justin felt jealous and found his perfectionism amped up when he saw a dynamic youth pastor with a growing ministry. What tempts you to compare and compete with others? Perhaps when you see someone who:

- Has a new outfit or a new car

- Has lots of money

- Is real attractive or has a dynamic personality

- Enjoys a great marriage or family life

- Is super successful

- Cuts in front of you on the road

Which of these situations bothers you? How do you react? Imagine resisting envy and ambition and instead being concerned for the other person's welfare (Philippians 2:3). Imagine that your normal reaction in these situations is to *cheerfully* bless your "competitor" with silent prayers or kind words.

Be Immersed in Jesus' Reality

To be able to freely bless people who have something we want or who hurt us in some way *we need more than will power.* It's not an easy yoke to smile through gritted teeth! To bless those who seem to be competing with us we need to experience a *baptism into the reality of God's heavenly kingdom that Jesus shows us.*[117] By "baptism" I mean more than getting wet while a pastor says, "I baptize you in the name of the Father, the Son, and the Spirit."

Names in the Bible reflect the *reality* behind them. *To be baptized is to be submerged in the Trinitarian presence.*[118]

The eternal waters of baptism are the living waters of God's Spirit, God's presence and power beside us right now as we're doing what we're doing. Immersing ourselves in the Trinitarian reality washes and renews us. It redefines our identity over time — forming us in the glorious image of Christ. We need this healing and renewal! We need to train to live in this baptismal.

Oh, to be submerged in God's love for us by experiencing that we are one with Christ!

A favorite meditation of mine that I often share with others is imagining being baptized with Jesus. (It helps that I've actually been baptized in the Jordan River!)

Let's visualize Matthew 3:13-17. Jesus is with John the Baptist and they're standing in the Jordan River. John baptizes him and he comes up out of the water...

The Holy Spirit in the form of a dove descends from the skies and lands on Jesus, remaining on his shoulder...

The Father God's voice rolls like thunder, powerful and deep, as he publicly affirms Jesus: "This is my beloved Son and in him I am well pleased."...

Now see yourself baptized, submerged not only in the water but also in the Trinitarian reality...

Be washed... Be renewed... Be embraced in the love of God... *You are in Christ!...*

As you come up out of the water imagine the Holy Spirit lands on *you* as a dove and he remains on you...

Listen as the Father is speaking to you and he wants everyone to hear: *"You* are my beloved son/daughter. In you I am well pleased..."

When we live under the reign of our Redeemer then we will not be controlled by anxiety, jealousy, or competitiveness. We'll be ready to bless and encourage others, even those who are difficult or who offend us because we're living in a different world than the one we see — it's a world where "God demonstrates his own love for us in this: While we were still sinners, Christ died for us" (Romans 5:8) and so "We love because [God] first loved us" (1 John 4:19).

Those who have learned to live securely in the Kingdom-yoke of Jesus are prepared to bless difficult people — freely and naturally, without pressure or condemnation and without being a doormat or someone who has no boundaries. They're so enjoying God's blessings that they're *overflowing* to others.

Blessings overflow from you when you're living in Jesus' Kingdom-yoke!

A Breath Prayer From the Bible

As I said before, early in my hiatus from writing books out of love for my family and the Lord I was tempted to be jealous of some of my colleagues. On one of these occasions the Holy Spirit taught me a little Scripture Prayer that greatly helped me and I've been using it ever since. It's based on Christ's "kenosis" or self-emptying love which we just discussed: "Do nothing out of selfish ambition or vain conceit, but in humility consider others better than yourselves... Let your attitude be the same as that of Christ Jesus" (Philippians 2:3, 5).

You can pray this for people who trigger jealousy or competitiveness in you or for those who mistreat you. It's a concrete discipline that can *put you in a posture to be transformed by God's grace to be more generous toward others.*

But, let me repeat my caution again: don't make the mistake of misusing Paul's words to heap onto yourself guilt and pressure! Paul is *not* saying, "You shouldn't *feel* jealous or ambitious. And shame on you if you do!" He is *not* saying, "Don't pay attention to your own needs — just treat other people well."

He's saying, "Look to the humble love of Christ to find your value and power." The Lord Almighty and King of kings left the glory of heaven, took on the limitations of human flesh, picked up a towel, got on his knees, and washed our dirty feet! (John 13:1-17). He serves us even though we don't deserve it! If we appreciate the gift of his mercy and kindness to us then we'll learn to share it with others in our attitude and actions: *we'll bless and serve others as he continually does for us.* (As we've emphasized, we also need to experience Christ's love from godly people.)

Let's try praying Philippians 2:3 as a Breath Prayer:

* As you inhale pray, "In Christ's humility…"

* As you exhale pray, "Consider others more than self…"

I like to add an initial waiting to breathe step to this rhythm and use hand motions to put more of my body into engaging my mind and heart with God's word. Here's how you can do this:

* Wait to breathe as you kneel before God quietly. Feel your longing for oxygen and for the Spirit. As you do this raise your hands high in worship of the Lord who humbly serves you…

* Then slowly breathe in the words, "In Christ's humility." As you pray pull your hands toward your chest, receiving Christ's generous, gracious, servant love…

- Then exhale the words, "Consider others more than self." As you do this extend your hands outward to overflow with Christ's consideration and esteem for others.

Also, here are some steps to target this prayer as a watch and pray discipline for your transformation in Christlikeness:

1. Continue your Breath Prayer rhythm with Philippians 2:3 until your body relaxes and you enjoy a sense of God's peace...

2. Identify someone who has been a competitor to you and visualize how you get tempted to jealousy, ambition, or competitiveness...

3. Return to repeating and enjoying the breathing prayer: "In Christ's humility... Consider others more than self."

4. Offer a prayer of blessing for this person...

5. Ask God to empower you to be kind in the future...

Soul Talk

Feeling like you're not _____ enough makes you susceptible to selfish ambition and envy. To break free it helps to share openly with someone who offers you Christ's compassion:

1. What do wildflowers tell you about Jesus' easy yoke?

2. What is an example of how you've felt inadequate, jealous, or competitive recently?

3. Did you offer words of blessing or a secret prayer for a competitor this week? How did it affect you?

Chapter Ten

"Fear Not!"

The starter's gun was about to fire to start the triathlon. It was time for a final gut check: Was I ready to dive in and face my fear of swimming? Could I finish a half-mile swim in the ocean?

I was standing on the beach with my 19-year old son and hundreds of other swimmers crammed like sardines on the beach and looking into an ocean of freezing water. I was shivering and I wasn't even wet yet! Six foot high waves, one after the other, were roaring towards me and I was going to have to swim through those crashing walls of salt water and go a quarter mile out to a buoy that I could barely see and then come back to shore.

Soon all the people around me would be pushing to get in front of me and splashing in the water. But I didn't care about being first — I just wanted to finish the race alive! *Really.* I had been told that recently a shark had eaten a person on that very beach! I tried to dismiss this thought as highly unlikely. But I worried, *How am I going to breathe with all the waves and splashes of water in my face? What if I start choking on salt water?*

For me to live is Christ and to die is gain...

One thing I do... I press on toward the goal to win the prize for which God has called me heavenward in Christ...

I have learned to be content whatever the circumstances. I know what it is to be in need, and I know what it is to have plenty... I can do everything through Christ who gives me strength" (Philippians 1:21, 3:13-14, 4:13).

I can overcome my fear through Christ who gives me strength... I can swim in this ocean through Christ who gives me strength...

Meditating on Paul's words helped me to "take courage" from my Lord. *Live or die* I was going to swim in the roaring ocean with Jesus! I was not going to shrink back! So when the gun sounded I dove into the ocean and started swimming for my medal!

But as I swam it was obvious that *I was struggling.* I took in a lot of salt water! I felt and looked like I was dog paddling as all the expert swimmers passed me up. In fact, along the swim route there were lifeguards sitting atop surfboards and separately two of them asked me, "Are you okay?" They were afraid I was going to drown! But I was praying as I swam, "I can do everything through Christ who gives me strength." The lifeguards didn't see that I was swimming with Jesus! (I'm still glad they were watching me!)

Assisted by God's grace, I finished the swim and my first triathlon. How did I do? For the swimming portion I came in 70th place out of 72 male swimmers my age! I did a lot better on the bike and the run, but beating other people was not the point — it was about diving in to face my fear with Jesus.

More than a fear of swimming, as I'll elaborate on later, I was about to leave a twenty year successful career and plunge headfirst into working full time as a missionary to pastors.

"There's No Safe Place"

We live in an age of terrorism that is spreading around the globe. ISIS and Al Qaida carry out public executions of innocent people. American citizens have shot to death kids in school and people praying in church. We see these things happen before our eyes on television and the Internet. Even our children see this.

Obviously, our world is not a safe place anymore. Or maybe it never was safe? Death has always been a thief that takes some people "before their time." Disease, abuse, tornadoes, and other hardships seem to strike people randomly.

These are just a few reasons of the reasons we have for being afraid, always anxious, even filled with dread. It's no wonder that we say to ourselves things like:

- "There's no safe place for me."
- "Don't get your hopes up."
- "It's weak to feel fear."
- "I deserve to be abused."
- "I'm too scared to try that."

But are these statements *really true?* Is it good to live afraid of bad things happening to you? Is it good to do the opposite and live in denial of bad things happening to you?

"The Lord is my refuge." In view of
so much evil where is that safe place?

It isn't just death, disease, and tragedy that we're afraid of — there are many fears and phobias that we may struggle with.

What Are Your Fears?

Every day thousands of people visit SoulShepherding.org and one of their top searches is for help with *fear*. What are we afraid of? I gathered a list of 16 of the most common fears and phobias.[119] In some cases they're just annoyances, but in other cases they're debilitating.

Which of these fears do you relate to? For each fear underline the word that best describes the extent to which it troubles you, ranging from "none" to "overwhelming."

1. Flying: None - Some - Problematic - Overwhelming

2. Public speaking: None - Some - Problematic - Overwhelming

3. Heights: None - Some - Problematic - Overwhelming

4. Darkness: None - Some - Problematic - Overwhelming

5. Intimacy: None - Some - Problematic - Overwhelming

6. Death or dying: None - Some - Problematic - Overwhelming

7. Failure: None - Some - Problematic - Overwhelming

8. Rejection: None - Some - Problematic - Overwhelming

9. Spiders: None - Some - Problematic - Overwhelming

10. Commitment: None - Some - Problematic - Overwhelming

11. Driving: None - Some - Problematic - Overwhelming

12. Dogs: None - Some - Problematic - Overwhelming

13. Dentists: None - Some - Problematic - Overwhelming

14. Snakes: None - Some - Problematic - Overwhelming

15. Needles: None - Some - Problematic - Overwhelming

16. Being alone: None - Some - Problematic - Overwhelming

It's normal to have some degree of fear with some of these issues, but if you're suffering with any fears that are restricting or overwhelming then you need help.

"Fear Not!" 365 Days a Year

All these things that cause us fear and anxiety and *yet the most repeated instruction in the Bible is "Fear not!"* In fact, it's been said that there are 365 "Fear nots" in the Bible — one for every day of the year! Lloyd Ogilvie in *Facing the Future without Fear* even said there are 366 "Fear nots" in the Bible, one for every day of the year, including Leap Year! God doesn't want us to go a single day without hearing his word of comfort, "Fear not!"

Actually, there are *way more* than 365 "Fear nots" in the Bible! Some Bible students tell me that's not true. Indeed, the King James Version says "Fear not" or "Be not afraid" 103 times. So why do I say that there are more than 365 "Fear nots" in the Bible?

"Fear" is spoken of *over 500 times* in the KJV. Furthermore, in addition to the "Fear nots" many times the Bible teaches us to

"Fear God," which really means reverence God alone and *do not fear anyone or anything else.* Expanding the search to look at verses encouraging us not to worry or not to be anxious would add many, many more "Fear not" Scriptures.

The most powerful and unforgettable "Fear not" of the Bible occurs in John 6:16-21. Jesus has just fed five thousand men with a few loaves and fishes. Then he made his disciples get in the boat to cross the lake while he went on the mountainside to pray. There he kept vigil all night and in the middle of the night a terrible storm arose and he could see them straining at the oars, fighting against the wind and waves and the driving rain. They were hardly able to move forward.

So Jesus came to them, *walking on the water!* When the disciples saw him they cried out in fear, thinking he was ghost! But Jesus spoke to them: "Take courage! It is I! Fear not!" (v 20, paraphrased) Then he climbed into the boat and the storm ceased, the lake became calm!

Mark says Jesus' cadre were confounded because their hearts were hardened — they had not understood when Jesus multiplied the loaves. If they'd known that Jesus could create bread by praying then they would've known that he also could walk on water! The Son of God was their friend — *they were safe with him in the kingdom of his Father.*

The Kingdom of Love is our secret, safe refuge — now and for eternity!

Perfect Love

It's natural to be afraid if you're in a little boat at sea that gets caught in a fierce storm. Even John Wesley, the 17th Century founder of the Methodists, was frightened when he was in a ship sailing on mission from England to America. But the Moravians who were also on the boat with him were *not* afraid — *they were joyful and peaceful as they sang hymns to the Lord!*

In danger the Moravians were relaxed like Jesus was in the Mark 4 and 6 storms at sea. They were calm because they knew that the Lord of the Seas was with them. Their Savior worked miracles! He'd risen from the dead! His word was sure: "Take courage! It is I! Fear not!" They rested in his love.

Seeing the Moravian's faith led Wesley from a life of Christian duty into a personalized salvation that ignited his faith in Christ and spread to *millions of people around the world.*

The Beloved Disciple of Jesus promises us, "Perfect love removes all fear" (1 John 4:18). There is profound psychology in this verse. Underneath any significant fear is the ultimate fear: *the fear of being abandoned or alone* (number 16 on the list above, but really it's number 1). All enduring fear comes from being disconnected from loving relationship. In the fruit of the Spirit joy and peace flow from love.

How can we experience the fullness of love that makes us secure and free from fear, even in the face of danger or death? Our Christian answer is that we need to trust in Jesus Christ for the forgiveness of our sins and eternal life in heaven. This is essential! And yet many born again Christians are overwhelmed with fear or anxiety. What's missing? Are we just lacking faith in the promises of the Bible?

We need *empathy.* We need to feel our emotions and internalize the compassion of someone who feels our distress, validates our emotion, and accepts us as we are. Empathy looks like active listening, staying interested, being emotionally present, asking good questions, reflecting feelings, being a faithful friend. "Rejoice with those who rejoice and mourn with those who mourn" (Romans 12:15) — that's empathy. That's God's perfect love flowing through a person to remove another's fear.

"Empathy is oxygen for the soul," I often say. Without continual access to empathy we become anxious and afraid.

Without empathy your soul is gasping for air!

To receive empathy we need to ask for it from someone gracious who has capacity and then receive it as a gift from God by *agreeing with it.* When a friend agrees to listen we think, *Yes, I need this.* Then we smile and say, "Thank you for listening."

The trials of life require that we keep seeking empathy, rather than denying our emotion or distracting ourselves. Unhealed emotional wounds of the past need healing. Self-condemning voices need to be hushed. We're learning how to bond emotionally with safe, compassionate people. We must persevere in prayer.

When empathy abides in us then it can flow out of us to others in need.

You Belong in the Trinitarian Family!

Let's meditate on the Trinity to secure and solidify our souls in fear-not-attachment. Here is the perfect family we long for!

The Father, Son, and Holy Spirit each are all-powerful and self-sustaining, enjoying fullness of life in their own selves. No member of the Trinity needs anything or has to answer to anybody, but will out of love each can choose to depend on or submit to one another or, within limits, even to lesser beings like you and I!

Consider the other-centered way that members of the Godhead rejoice to relate to each other: Father, Son, and Spirit take turns shining the spotlight on one another. The Father sends us the gift of the Holy Spirit and Jesus breathes the Spirit into us.

And the Spirit calls out in our hearts, "Papa Father!" and "Jesus is Lord." Back and forth they love and praise one another! The Father thunders from heaven, "Jesus is my beloved son and in him I am well pleased" and the Spirit lights on him in the form of a dove. And Jesus replies that the Father is the greatest and warns us never to speak a word against the Holy Spirit.

Then God comes to us in the incarnation of Christ. The King of kings comes as a servant. Our Lord was born in a smelly barn, laid in an animal feeding trough, raised by a poor family in a tiny village, worked as an obscure carpenter, went into public ministry as a nomad, was rejected by friends and neighbors, and crucified as a criminal. Jesus Christ is Immanuel, God with us and through his perfect life, sacrificial death on the cross, and resurrection from the dead he reconciles us to God.

In view of the cross we see that God stoops down to make *us* great! (Psalm 18:35). The whole Trinity comes to us. The Father shares his glory with us (John 17:22). The Lord Jesus comes with a towel to wash our feet (John 13:1-17). The Spirit that raised Jesus from the dead comes to live in us (Romans 8:11).

When we appreciate the Three-Personed God's humble generosity it removes our fear and impels us to give up our self-centered ways and share his blessings with others. So we shine the spotlight on God and we honor one another above ourselves.

You're Invited to the Dance!

Maybe you know the experience of not being invited to the Homecoming Dance? Or being one the last people picked for a team?

It hurts to be left out! And when we experience this enough times we come to believe, *That's who I am — unwanted. I'm a reject.* Tragically, this belief becomes a self-fulfilling prophecy in which the person who feels eligible to be rejected unconsciously finds judgmental or fickle people and evokes rejection from them.

It's a vicious cycle that can leave us depressed and continually afraid of more rejection.

We all need to know that we're seen, heard, and wanted; we need to experience that people are glad to see us. This is how God feels about you.[120] Picture it like the Supreme and Sweet Society of the Three says to you: "Come on in! Join our dance!"

A dance with the Trinity? Yes! Eugene Peterson says that in approaching the Trinity we can visualize a square dance that we're invited to join. His vision, which goes back to fourth century monks, is that Father, Son, and Spirit are giving and responding to one another in a celebratory love dance that we're invited to join.[121]

It's in this spirit that the Psalmist prays to God, "Oh, visit the earth, ask her to join the dance!... Surprise us with love at daybreak; then we'll skip and dance all the day long... Your revelation is the tune I dance to" (Psalm 65:9, 90:14, 119:77; MSG). The Apostle Paul sees the dance too. He urges us, "Keep on doing what we told you to do to please God, not in a dogged religious plod, but in a living, spirited dance" (1 Thessalonians 4:1, MSG).

Lord of the dance, deliver us
from the dogged religious plod!

Fear, anxiety, and guilt can take us into trudging along in a dogged religious plod with reading our Bible, going to church, and serving others just because we should, even though our heart isn't it. That's stressing out over getting all the dance steps, sequences, and movements right — I've done that and it's no fun!

If you're in a dogged religious plod and need to start dancing with the Trinity then it might be a time to back off from standard spiritual disciplines and demanding ministry to others. More Bible reading, more prayer, more church attendance, and more serving probably aren't the answer. Maybe you need to seek empathy from compassionate people and learn to have fun with Jesus. He's ready to listen to you and show you how to dance in the "Father and Son intimacies" and delight in their "unforced rhythms of grace."

Face Your Fear

Dancing with Jesus is not how most us react to difficult challenges! Commonly we avoid them. *But this weakens us!* When you keep avoiding a situation that you're afraid of or stressed by, it provides momentary relief, but in the end it actually strengthens your fear. Some people will develop panic disorder or embarrassing phobias by not dealing with their fear. *But the way to be free of anxiety is to face your fears in Jesus' yoke of love.*

To be in Jesus' yoke is an
easy way of doing hard things.

For instance, if you're afraid of driving on the road you can seek emotional support from someone you trust. This may involve facing a fear of embarrassment, but you can take courage and ask for empathy and prayer from a friend or counselor. Talk about how it feels to drive. In fact, go on an imaginary drive and relay your experiences. As you do this, take comfort and confidence from your friend and from the Lord. Then *go drive your car!* That's how to overcome fear.

In 2009 Kristi and I started Soul Shepherding, Inc. as a 501c3 nonprofit ministry to pastors. Just over one year later we gave up most of our outside income and became dependent on donations and whatever pastors could pay us for services. It was the biggest step of faith in God that we'd ever taken!

I had resisted making this move for a number of years — despite Ray Ortlund's example and encouragement. I was afraid of failure and rejection (numbers seven and eight on the above list of Most Common Fears). But then God spoke to my heart on a long prayer hike in the hills: "Bill, there are people that would want to help you if you would let them."

But Lord, I don't want to be constantly asking people for money! On top of that we were mired in the worst economy since the Great Depression! I was too scared. I refused to follow the Lord's call for another year. I paid the price of being increasingly overloaded with the stress of working as a Spiritual Formation Pastor in a church, seeing therapy clients, and ministering to pastors from other churches on the side. Worse, I felt my faith shrinking and I knew that I was missing out on what God wanted us to do.

Finally, we dove in and faced our fear! But we didn't do this alone. The Lord directed us to gather with a group of friends and family who loved us and our ministry. There were two pastors in this group. We were vulnerable and opened our hearts and lives to them. They listened, empathized, prayed, and believed in God's call on us. They supported us taking the plunge!

Eight years later I am amazed, not only at how God helped us overcome our fears, but at how how he has grown the outer reach of Soul Shepherding to surpass *one million* webpage views per year. It all started with The Apprentice Prayer which culminates with: "Today, I'm ready to lead people to follow you, Jesus. Amen."

Experiment

Healing Prayer For Harmful Images

For our last experiment I want to share with you a powerful way of praying that has helped me with so many things, including facing my fear of serving full time in a nonprofit ministry: *visualizing Jesus as he's revealed in the Gospels.*

The power of images is *vastly under appreciated* by most Christians. Images that we internalize carry emotion. They facilitate an enduring attachment — to our betterment or detriment.

Imagining Jesus as he's revealed in the Bible is not a spiritual trick, wishful thinking, making an idol, or changing history — *it's tapping into the spiritual reality of the Only Begotten Son who was, is, and is to come.* It's a way of standing on Scriptural authority and the experiential foundation of our empathy-filled attachments with people in the Body of Christ and then reaching up with faith to the supernatural God in our midst.

In my case, as I dealt with anxiety and fear about taking a huge risk and changing my career I found great comfort and encouragement from the Father by filling my mind with Biblical images. This includes simple things like the smile of Jesus, God's hand reaching down from heaven, the cross, or Jesus' embrace.

For example, when Kristi and I shared the vision of Soul Shepherding with prospective investors we visualized taking hold the hand of the Lord. We refused to accept any pressure or to try to get people to do anything, but we also refused to hide from having conversations with people about our ministry. With each person or group we talked to we took hold of the heavenly hand of grace and *sought to serve people.* We didn't want anyone to give to our ministry unless it would bless them to do so and that's how we prayed. We trusted God and watched him provide abundantly more than we could've asked or imagined (Ephesians 3:20).

Damaged By Intrusive Images

Often what holds us back from stepping out in faith is a deep emotional insecurity related to painful memories. Abuse. Abandonment. Being distressed or in need, yet feeling that no one understands how you feel. Hurtful things said or done under the influence of alcohol or drugs. Frightening scenes from a movie. Pornographic images. Regret for bad choices. Angry explosions. The list goes on.

What do you do with these harmful memories and images? Maybe like Jessica was molested by her father (Chapter Four) we try to forget. We try not to feel. But this means becoming more emotionally detached, less alive, and less able to empathize with others.

When we've absorbed a harmful visual scene it can wreck havoc in our mind and body. We need to experience the "washing of the word" that God offers (Ephesians 5:26). We need positive, Biblical images and symbols to fill our thoughts and our emotions and to strengthen us to share God's peace and wisdom with others. (Philippians 4:8). We need prayer ministry from a soul shepherd.

Use the word of God like a miracle washcloth
that scrubs your mind clean of unhealthy images.

Recently Kristi and I were driving in Mexico to minister to the network of pastors there that we've adopted and we got stuck in a traffic jam. Two hours later we came to police cars and the scene of an accident. On the road I saw the bloody remains of a man next to his motorcycle. My stomach felt sick. I began to pray that he had trusted Christ and was in heaven and to pray for his family and friends.

But I couldn't get the image of what I saw out of my mind — nor the feeling of wanting to vomit or crawl out of my skin! Even a week later and after sharing my emotions with Kristi and asking God to free me I was still experiencing intrusive and upsetting recollections. I kept praying for the man and his loved ones, but now I needed special prayer!

Good Shepherd provided a meditative prayer experience that relieved my distress and redeemed the traumatic image. I found the exercise in a book that Kristi recommended to me: *Experiencing Healing Prayer* by Rick Richardson.[122]

As I went through this prayer process the Spirit of Jesus went with me to the scene of the accident and I saw the dead body but immediately it was changed: *It became white and filled with glorious light and it rose up to heaven!* This was my prayer for this man and the people who are grieving his death!

This God-blessed image has stayed! When the tragic and awful scene comes back to me I see God's redemption of it. Instead of being distressed I feel at peace. Instead of being frustrated by an intrusive image I'm thankful to pray for the man's loved ones.

Trust Christ to Free You of Bad Images

I'd like to share with you the healing prayer process that God used to cleanse my mind of that painful image and to release the man who died to God. You can follow these steps of prayer not only for intrusive images, but also for painful memories or patterns of emotional stuckness.[123]

1. *Set aside about 30 minutes for prayer.* Find a beautiful, secluded spot in nature or a quiet chair in your home where you can pray and open your heart to the Lord.

2. *Give thanks and praise to the Lord Jesus.* Using a favorite Scripture helps.

3. *Consecrate your imagination to God.* Ask the Lord to set you free from harmful images and memories. Ask him to fill your mind and your whole being with pictures that are true and lovely and encouraging.

4. *Ask God to show you an image or memory that needs healing.* It might be a hurtful scene from your childhood, a violent episode in a movie, a lustful image, something frightening you experienced, or a memory of emotional wounding.

5. *Imagine Jesus.* You might see him on the cross or risen from the dead and shining in glory. You might see him with his hands or arms open to you. You might recall a Gospel scene and see Jesus ministering to you in that way.

6. *Ask the Lord to help you "pull out" the harmful image(s) from your mind.* To help you pray use your hand to symbolically grab out each polluting picture that you recall.

7. *Look at Christ Jesus and listen.* Open your mind to the Holy Spirit to receive *a new and redemptive image.* You might see Jesus get rid of the bad image in some way. Or you might see him minister his love to you in a personal way.

You'll probably need to repeat this Scripture prayer process and you may need support from a counselor or prayer minister. This is because God has made us as relational beings and just as our wounds usually come from people so also we need to participate in "love one another" relationships in the Body of Christ to overcome our hurts and dysfunctions. Consider asking the Lord for a compassionate intercessor or counselor.

A Breath Prayer From the Bible

We love Jesus' words: "Peace I leave with you; my peace I give you. I do not give to you as the world gives. Do not let your hearts be troubled and do not be afraid" (John 14:27).

But maybe we don't appreciate the context of this promise. Jesus is saying, "Face your fears with my help." It's only when we take Jesus at his word and step out into a stressful situation with faith in him that *The Strengthener* (the Holy Spirit) comes to encourage us, helping us to make our home in the love of the Father and Son, in the spiritual reality that transcends our physical circumstances (John 14:23-27).

Jesus is offering us his *shalom*. Shalom is a Hebrew word that means "fullness." Full of life. Full of God's presence. So full that you're overflowing with love, joy, and peace! (They are all parts of the same "fruit," Galatians 5:22-23.) Shalom is what Jesus experienced during the storm at sea, when interrogated by religious scholars, and when standing before Pilate on trial to be crucified. Shalom is what enables you to experience stress without internalizing it and becoming worried and anxious.

You can try my "Shalom Prayer" to help you face your fears. It's inspired by Jesus' words in John 14:27. It will help you to be present to God, his Word and Spirit, if you breathe the words in and out. (We're using the rhythm that inhaling represents receiving and exhaling represents renouncing.)

- Peace of Christ... Not of this world

- Kingdom of God... Not of this world

- Fullness of God... Not of this world

- Wholeness and health... Not of this world

- Shalom... Not of this world

Rest secure in God's non-anxious, loving presence...

Then watch and pray with Jesus by calling to mind something you're afraid of, worried about, or challenged by. (This is a first step for facing your fear.)

Then return to the Shalom Prayer as a way of taking hold the hand of mercy that reaches down from the heavens — now and in the time of trial.

You can also use the Shalom prayer to intercede for a friend or family member who is struggling with fear.

Soul Talk

Sharing your insights and experiences with "Fear Not" can help you to face and overcome your fears and worries.

1. What is a fear that you struggle with? What helps you to deal with this?

2. How did it feel for you to meditate on the Trinity?

3. What was your experience with visualizing Jesus, praying for help with a harmful image, or doing the Shalom Prayer?

Easy Yoke Sermons or Small Groups

Your Best Life In Jesus' Easy Yoke is a curriculum for Christlikeness that's designed for you to share with your church, staff, class, or small group. Each chapter or week emphasizes the person of Christ, God's Word, and spiritual disciplines to apply the material to the test of real life. If you need a shorter time frame than ten weeks (one for each chapter) for your series of messages here are two suggested outlines of four or five weeks:

Apprenticeship to Christ (It's An Easy Yoke Life)

1. The Gospel of Jesus: Matthew 4:17, 5:1-12 (Chapters 1-2)

2. Trusting God in Trials: Mark 4:35-41 (Chapters 3-5)

3. Easy Yoke Power: John 15:1-15 (Chapters 6-7)

4. Love One Another: John 13:1-17 (Chapters 8-10)

A Non-Anxious Life (In Jesus' Easy Yoke)

1. Relax With Jesus: Matthew 11:25-30 (Chapter 1)

2. Abandon Outcomes to God: Philippians 4:4-7 (Chapters 2-3)

3. See Yourself as God Does: Luke 15:11-32 (Chapters 4-5)

4. Grace For Perfectionists: Matthew 6:25-34 (Chapters 6-7)

5. Fearless: John 6:16-21 (Chapters 8-10)

Endnotes

1 All Bible quotations are from the New International Version (1984 or 2011 edition), unless indicated otherwise. Other versions cited: MSG is The Message, NLT is New Living Translation, ESV is English Standard Version, KJV is King James Version, NKJV is New King James Version, NASB is New American Standard Bible, and AMP is Amplified Bible.

2 Personal notes from a conversation with Dallas Willard on December 31, 2010.

3 Ray Ortlund, Sr.'s book, Lord, Make My Life a Miracle! (Regal Books: 1974), is filled with his enthusiastic insights on living for Christ, loving one another, and reaching the world with the Gospel.

4 "Apprentice" is a term that Dallas Willard uses for disciple. Sadly, our understanding today of discipleship to Jesus has become quite watered down. Apprenticeship to Jesus is concrete and practical; it emphasizes that we learn from being with Jesus and working side-by-side with him over a long period of time.

It used to be that to be a "Christian" was to be a disciple of Jesus. In fact, in the New Testament the word "Christian" is only used three times and the word "disciple" is used 269 times! The New Testament was written by disciples of Jesus, for disciples of Jesus, about discipleship to Jesus. All the promises of the New Testament are for disciples of Jesus. See "Discipleship: For Super Christians Only" by Dallas Willard in his books The Spirit of the Disciplines (Harper: 1988), pp. 258-265 and The Great Omission (Harper: 2006, pp. 3-12.)

5 These are the dynamics of a person that Jesus identified in the Greatest Commandment (Mark 12:29-31). Dallas Willard teaches that your heart is the core of your being and refers to your intentions and choices. Your soul is your personality from the inside out, the flow of your being. Your mind includes your thoughts, ideas, images, and feelings. Your strength is your body and energy. Your relationships include all the social interactions and ties you have with people. He explains that each function of your self needs to be understood and it needs to interact with God's grace-giving Word and Spirit for healing and growth so that your whole person can be transformed to be more like Jesus. See his "Circle Diagram" in Renovation of the Heart (Navpress: 2002) p. 38

6 Dallas Willard didn't want to be called "Dr. Willard" or even "Professor." He said, "Just call me Dallas." He exalted God and humbled himself in the manner that Jesus taught (Matthew 23:8-12). By the way, he was named after the county he was born in: Dallas, Missouri.

7 Personal notes from a conversation with Dallas Willard on September 26, 2007.

8 See Dallas Willard's books, Hearing God, The Spirit of the Disciplines, The Divine Conspiracy, Renovation of the Heart, The Great Omission, and Knowing Christ Today. Also DWillard.org has a section of Dallas' seminars on CD.

9 "Relax with Jesus" by Bill Gaultiere (SoulShepherding.org: 2014) is a Bible study that includes more examples of Jesus ministering his non-anxious presence.

10 Personal notes from a conversation with Dallas Willard on September 26, 2007.

11 Author's paraphrase from John 10:10.

12 You can sign up to receive these free weekly devotional emails at SoulShepherding.org.

13 The Triangle of Soul Transformation is adapted from Dallas Willard's "Golden Triangle of Spiritual Growth," which focuses on (1) The Action of the Holy Spirit, (2) Ordinary Events of Life: Temptations, and (3) Planned Disciplines to Put on a New Heart. Each are centered in the mind of Christ (See *The Divine Conspiracy,* p. 347). See also "Adopting the Narratives of Jesus" by James Bryan Smith, *The Good and Beautiful God: Falling in Love With The God Jesus Knows,* (IVP: 2009) p. 24.

14 Author's paraphrase and elaboration of Matthew 4:17.

15 James Bryan Smith, *The Good and Beautiful God.* Smith identifies "false narratives" that undermine trust in Jesus' gospel of the kingdom.

16 Internalizing and imitating Christ go together. You can't imitate him without receiving and relying on his Spirit. At the same time, if you think you've taken in the Spirit of Jesus, but you're not becoming like him you need help learning to truly trust Christ with your heart.

17 "Lectio Divina Groups" by Bill Gaultiere (SoulShepherding.org: 2010, 2008) discusses Lectio Divina's history and rhythms. It also features applications for small groups and private devotions.

18 Eugene Peterson, *The Message* (Navpress:1993). Portions of Peterson's paraphrase of Matthew 11:25-30 will be quoted throughout this book without citing the reference.

19 "Lectio Divina Guides" by Bill Gaultiere on (SoulShepherding.org: 2012) includes an archive of over sixty PDF's, each is one page and free. They feature a Bible passage on a spiritual formation theme, brief introduction, Breath Prayer, the text, and reflection questions with space for journaling.

20 The bracketed text are easy yoke phrasing imported from traditional translations.

21 "Breath Prayers" by Bill Gaultiere (SoulShepherding.org: 2010, 2006) discusses the Biblical and Christian history of this discipline and instructions for using various breathing and meditation rhythms. (See also "Breath Prayers From the Bible.")

22 This is not her real name and certain details have been changed. This is the pattern throughout this book.

23 Frances de Sales, *An Introduction to the Devout Life* (Vintage: 2002; originally published in 1609), pp. 202-204. During the Protestant Reformation de Sales brought reform within the Catholic Church.

24 In 1979 after a born again experience Bob Dylan composed his famous song "You Gotta Serve Somebody." It was part of his album "Slow Train Coming."

25 Matthew 11:28-30, author's paraphrase.

26 Dallas Willard writes, "Currently we are not only saved by grace: we are paralyzed by it." *The Great Omission: Reclaiming Jesus' Essential Teachings on Discipleship* (Harper: 2006). p. 166. The insights on grace that follow are from Dallas.

27 Dallas Willard in *The Spirit of the Disciplines* (Harper: 1998) teaches that the key to transformation in Christlikeness is practicing spiritual disciplines in order to live in the easy yoke of Jesus.

28 Dallas Willard, *The Spirit of the Disciplines.*

29 Richard Foster writes in *Celebration of Discipline* (Harper & Row: 1978), "By themselves the Spiritual Disciplines can do nothing; they can only get us to the place where something can be done. They are God's means of grace" (p. 6).

30 *Ibid,* pp. 97-98.

31 Matthew 26:54; Mark 14:49; Luke 4:21; John 17:12, 19:24, 19:28, 19:36.

32 Dallas Willard, *Renovation of the Heart* (Navpress: 2002), pp. 135, 150-152.

33 Ray Ortlund teaches "shooting up little arrow prayers to God" to grow in a life of peace and power. Brother Lawrence (1611-1691) called this "Practicing God's Presence."

34 Psychiatrists Thomas Holmes and Richard Rahe developed the "Holmes and Rahe Stress Scale" in 1967 after examining the medical records of over 5,000 patients to determine if stressful events cause illnesses. They found a positive correlation, as has subsequent research. This test is slightly modified (e.g., the dollar amounts).

35 The story of Abraham's friendship with God and brining Isaac to the altar of the Lord is told in Genesis 22:1-19, Hebrews 11:17-19, and James 2:21-24.

36 Jesus endured trials with peace, joy, and love: working as an ordinary carpenter and serving difficult customers, losing his father at a young age, having his ministry rejected by his family and hometown friends, religious leaders and unruly crowds trying to kill him, people mocking him, disciples turning away from him, and constant ministry pressure.

37 Dallas Willard, *The Divine Conspiracy* (Harper: 1997).

38 Matthew uses the term "kingdom of the heavens" rather than "kingdom of God" to emphasize the direct and immediate availability of the Lord's rule. We capitalize these terms in *Easy Yoke* to highlight that the Kingdom of God is a real place for us to live. Also, "Heavens" is put in the plural because that's the literal translation in the Bible. (See Young's Literal Translation on BibleGateway.com.) The Hebrew concept in the Bible is that there are levels to the heavens and the lowest one is in the air we breathe.

39 Eugene Peterson, *The Jesus Way: A Conversation on the Ways that Jesus is the Way* (Eerdmans: 2007). In the first century Church disciples of Jesus were known as followers of "the Way" (Acts 9:2; 19:9, 23; 24:14, 22).

40 Dallas Willard writes, "If you ask evangelicals to pick the smartest man in the world, very few of them will list Jesus Christ... How can you be a disciple of someone you don't think of as really bright?" *The Great Omission:* (Harper: 2006), p. 168.

41 These three points correspond to the Triangle of Soul Transformation in Chapter One.

42 William Law, *A Serious Call to a Devout and Holy Life* (Westminster John Knox Press: 1955; originally written in 1728), p. 101. John Wesley called this one of the three books which accounted for his first "explicit resolve to be all devoted to God." Law established an informal Protestant monastic fellowship, which he lived in the last 21 years of his life.

43 Most of the insights on the beatitudes in this chapter are from Dallas Willard's *The Divine Conspiracy* (Chapter 4).

44 Dallas Willard, "The Jesus Conspiracy," Serrano Hills Church in Tustin, CA, 2009.

45 Jesus surely learned The Magnificat from his mother as a boy. We know he studied the Great Reversals of the Old Testament. Probably meditating on these over the years inspired his beatitudes.

46 Dallas Willard, *The Divine Conspiracy* (Harper: 1997), p. 123.

47 "Jesus' Beatitudes for Pastors" by Bill Gaultiere (SoulShepherding.org: 2014) gives a number of examples of applying the Kingdom of God proclamations of blessing to church ministry.

48 Dallas Willard, *The Divine Conspiracy*, p. 116.

49 "Blessed" by Paul Simon and Art Garfunkle in their 1966 hit album, "Sounds of Silence."

50 Bill Gaultiere, "The God Image Questionnaire" (SoulShepherding.org: 2014; originally from a Ph.D. dissertation in 1989, revised in 2000.)

51 A. W. Tozer, *The Knowledge of the Holy* (HarperCollins: 1961), pp. 1-2. Tozer was a Christian Missionary & Alliance pastor and author of 40 Christian books. He never attended Bible college or seminary, but was Spirit-taught and Spirit-filled to become a man who loved and served Christ with unrelenting passion.

52 Dr. Foster was the head of internal medicine at the Southwestern Medical School, University of Texas. He told this story in a message he gave at First Presbyterian Church of Dallas, TX in 1999. (FirstPresDallas.org)

53 "Bible Verses on the Father's Love" and "God's Love Letter to You" by Bill Gaultiere are compilations of affirming Bible verses. (SoulShepherding.org: 2010; originally 2001 and 2003)

54 Brennan Manning, *Stranger to Self-Hatred* (Dimension Books: 1982), p. 40. Brennan was a friar and priest, appreciated as much by Evangelicals as Catholics. He struggled with alcoholism and depression in his life, which drove him deeper into his love-relationship with Jesus and his Abba and gave him great compassion for the hurts of other people.

55 Brennan Manning, *Abba's Child* (Navpress: 1994)

56 Bobby Schuller is the pastor of Hour of Power. In his book *Happiness According to Jesus* he shares fresh insights and applications from the Sermon on the Mount (Worthy Books: 2015).

57 Bill Gaultiere, "Biblical Blunders that Bruise and Confuse" (SoulShepherding.org: 2014, 2007).

58 Jesus also said, "The last shall be first and the first shall be last" (Matthew 20:16; see also Matthew 19:30 and Mark 9:35), "The greatest among you will be your servant" (Matthew 23:11; see also Matthew 20:26), and "Those who exalt themselves will be humbled, and those who humble themselves will be exalted" (Matthew 23:12).

59 Author's paraphrases from Psalms 8:4-5 and 139:6-7, 17.

60 Ray Ortlund, *Lord, Make My Life a Miracle!*, p. 40.

61 *Ibid*, p. 23.

62 This list includes when Paul uses the wording "in him" or "in the Lord."

63 Aelred of Rievaulx, *Spiritual Friendship* (University of Scranton Press: 1994, originally published in 1157), p. 29. Aelred was a Cistercian monk in the middle ages. He wrote during a time when friendship was viewed with caution in the Church. He shows spiritual friendship to be both an expression of God's love and a path to know God's love. His book is a journal of the spiritually intimate conversations he had with his friend.

64 Luke 7:36-50.

65 Brennan Manning, *Stranger to Self-Hatred*, pp. 33-34.

66 *Ibid*, pp. 40, 42.

67 The Desert Fathers and Mothers of the third century used the Jesus Prayer to help them "pray without ceasing" (1 Thessalonians 5:17). It comes from the Psalmist's recurring cry, "Lord, have mercy on me" and the tax collector's prayer for mercy in Luke 18:13. "The Jesus Prayer: The Anonymous Pilgrim's Story" by Bill Gaultiere (SoulShepherding.org: 2010) tells the story of the Anonymous Russian Pilgrim of the 19th Century and how he was physically healed and spiritually transformed by continually praying the Jesus Prayer.

68 Martin Luther, *A Simple Way to Pray* (Westminster John Knox Press: 2000, originally published in 1535), p. 56.

69 Bill Gaultiere, "Electric Bible Passages For Scripture Memory" (Soulshepherding.org: 2012). This article features a list of recommended chapters and long passages to memorize, including those on Dallas Willard's list. He says that all Scripture is inspired by God and authoritative to guide our lives, but some of it is *electric!*

70 *Ibid.* The list of electric Scriptures includes Romans 8 and a link to a PDF of a "condensed version" of the chapter using key verses from the NIV84.

71 Archibald Hart, *The Hidden Link Between Adrenaline and Stress* (Word: 1991).

72 Consider how technological "time saving devices" complicate our lives or how we just flip a switch to extend our work day. We've largely lost our connection to the relaxing and natural rhythms of sunset and sunrise.

73 Alan Fadling, *An Unhurried Life* (IVP: 2013). See also Alan's blog AnUnhurriedLife.org.

74 There were 120 disciples that followed Jesus' parting instructions to wait for the coming Holy Spirit (Acts 1:15). These are the ones God especially used to birth the Church.

75 Author's paraphrases from Matthew 6:4, Matthew 20:26, Mark 9:35, Luke 6:38, Matthew 10:42, Luke 10:37, Matthew 25:34-36, John 13:14, Matthew 18:5, Matthew 22:39, Luke 6:27-28, Matthew 5:40-41, Matthew 25:40.

76 Thérèse of Lisieux felt called by God at the age of 14 to dedicate her life to Jesus. She became a nun one year later, joining her two older sisters in the enclosed Carmelite community of Lisieux, Normandy. Nine years later in 1897 she became ill and died of tuberculosis at the age of 24. Because of her sweet, humble love for God and neighbor she became known as "The Little Flower of Jesus" and one of the greatest saints of her era.

77 Richard Foster, *Prayer* (Harper: 1992), p. 62.

78 John Ortberg tells this story in his article, "Taking Care of Busyness" in Leadership Magazine, Fall 1998 and in his book, *The Life you've Always Wanted: Spiritual Disciplines for Ordinary People* (Zondervan: 2002), p. 76.

79 Gary M. Burge, *Jesus, the Middle Eastern Storyteller* (Zondervan: 2009), p. 26.

80 Sirach 19:29-30. From the Jewish apocrypha written in the second century BC (this is considered a Deuterocanonical book by Protestants). Edited for gender neutral language.

81 Paraphrases from Matthew 16:27 (MSG), Matthew 15:10, Matthew 11:15, Matthew 6:25-27, Luke 24:36, John 12:35, Mark 4:39 (NKJV), Mark 6:31 (NASB), Luke 10:38-42, Matthew 26:41, Mark 13:33 (AMP), Luke 18:1, Acts 1:4, Luke 10:36-37.

82 Joan Chittister, OSB, *Wisdom Distilled from the Daily: Living the Rule of St. Benedict Today* (Harper Collins: 1990), pp. 176-178.

83 C. S. Lewis, *Mere Christianity* (Harper: 2001, originally published in 1952), p. 198.

84 George Mueller (1805-1898) was an English evangelist and philanthropist who established many orphanages. Italics added. Edited for gender neutral language.

85 Bill Gaultiere, "Praying a Psalm in its Nature Setting" (SoulShepherding.org: 2010, 2009). This article features instructions for praying particular Psalms in nature settings like those described in the psalm itself.

86 Research has shown that some people have a taste for alcohol and the capacity to drink more than most people and so they're more vulnerable to become alcoholics. Others are that way with work. Their feelings of inadequacy push them to overwork and no matter how much success they achieve it never brings them peace and confidence.

87 Blaise Pascal (1623-1662), Pensées #136 published in 1670. Quoted in *Christianity for Modern Pagans: Pascal's Pensées* (Ignatius Press: 1993), p. 172. Edited for gender neutral language.

88 Martin Luther (1483-1546), *A Simple Way to Pray* (Westminster John Knox Press: 2000, originally published in 1535), pp. 18-19.

89 Fourteen times in The Message Eugene Peterson uses the phrase "inside out." (BibleGateway.com)

90 This was taught in "The Journey," a two-year spiritual formation, leadership, and direction training program. To learn more visit SpiritualLeadership.com.

91 Paul Jensen, *Subversive Spirituality* (Pickwick Publications: 2009), pp. 84-89.

92 Eugene Peterson, *Working the Angles* (Eerdmans: 1987), pp. 74-75.

93 For instance see Matthew 12:9-14, Luke 13:10-16, and John 5:1-15.

94 Psalm 127 is a great example of the importance of sleep and it's connection to Sabbath. It teaches us that getting enough sleep is a way of practicing our trust in God's provision. Also it helps us to be more loving to our children and others. This is one of the Psalms that the Israelites sang as they walked together on their Sabbath pilgrimages to Jerusalem.

95 John Woolman (1720-1772) was a devout Quaker writer and itinerant preacher in the American colonies. He was also a successful tailor. He led the movement to abolish slavery, though it didn't succeed in his lifetime. Thomas Kelly references Woolman sending customers to his competitors in *A Testament of Devotion* (Harper: 1941), pp. 93-94.

96 Eugene Peterson, *Working the Angles* (Eerdmans: 1987), pp. 74-75. He says the Sabbath Psalmist (Psalm 92) provides us with three metaphors showing that the parallel Sabbath actions of praying and playing are like music (verses 1-4), animals (verses 10-11), and palm trees (verses 12-14). Music? Animals? Palm trees? Yes! Praying and playing need the musician's combination of discipline and delight, the wild ox's unrestrained and exuberant prancing, and the palm tree's vibrant growth in the desert. And because prayerful play and playful prayer are not meant to be detached from real-world-living the middle of the Sabbath Psalm also addresses how we overcome the problem of evil (verses 5-9).

97 Dallas Willard had a message called "How Many Birds are you Worth?"

98 Elizabeth Cheney, *Streams in the Desert* (Zondervan: 1996, originally published in 1925), October 10th devotional.

99 Zephaniah 3:17 is a wonderful promise for the Lord's people! "The LORD your God is with you, he is mighty to save. He will take great delight in you, he will quiet you with his love, he will rejoice over you with singing."

100 Hope, love, joy, and peace may seem to be feelings, but Dallas Willard says that along with faith they are "states of being" or character traits that include emotion, but primarily have to do with our mindset and orientation of will. They're also part of our bodies and profoundly affect our social relations. See *Renovation of the Heart* (Navpress: 2002), pp. 117-139.

101 Henry Cloud and John Townsend, *Boundaries* (Zondervan: 1992). The authors integrate the Bible and psychology and offer many practical examples of how to develop good personal boundaries.

102 Dallas Willard, *Renovation of the Heart* (Navpress, 2002). He discusses these Biblical functions of a person at length.

103 In the 1980's it was learned that alcoholics typically had people who "enabled" them to drink irresponsibly. These "Co-Dependents" get emotionally enmeshed with the addict, deny their own needs and emotions, pay the price themselves for the addict's dysfunctional behavior, and compulsively try to fix the addict's problems. Helpful recovery programs include Al-Anon, Codependents Anonymous, and Celebrate Recovery.

104 Gossip and slander are boundary violations of others. Jesus teaches us to go directly to the person who has offended us and talk the issue through privately. Then if that doesn't work we're to bring someone along to help us resolve the conflict (Matthew 18:15-17).

105 Bill Gaultiere, "Codependency Recovery" (SoulShepherding.org: 2010, 2005).

106 Bill Gaultiere, "Jesus Set Boundaries" (SoulShepherding.org: 2010, 1998).

107 Thomas Kelly, *A Testament of Devotion* (HarperCollins: 1941), p. 91. Kelly experienced a personal revival after asking friends to join him in a small group in which they read and prayed from the classic books of Christian devotion.

108 *Ibid*, p, 93.

109 *Ibid*, pp. 91-92, 95, 96.

110 Secrecy is the practice of doing your good deeds quietly, for God alone. See "Spiritual Disciplines List" by Bill Gaultiere (SoulShepherding.org: 2012).

111 Author's paraphrase of John 12:24.

112 These four meanings of "word" in the Bible are identified by Dallas Willard in *Hearing God* (IVP:1999), p. 142.

113 Jeanne Guyon, *Experiencing the Depths of Jesus Christ* (SeedSowers: 1981; originally published as *A Short and Very Easy Method of Prayer* in 1685). Her book evoked immediate controversy in the Catholic Church: stirring many in France to greater devotion to Christ, but leading to persecution and book burnings by the religious authorities. Her book went on to become one of the most widely read devotional books of all time, influencing both ordinary folk and great Christian leaders like John Wesley.

114 *Ibid*, pp. 2-4.

115 Bill Gaultiere, "Jesus Jujitsu: The Power to Turn the Other Cheek." This is a seminar on learning how to bless those that curse you (SoulShepherding.org: 2010, 2005).

116 For further discussion of this discipline see the section on "Soul Training: Praying for the Success of Competitors" in *The Good and Beautiful Life: Putting on the Character of Christ* by James Bryan Smith (IVP: 2009), pp. 135-136.

117 Mark 1:1-15 tells the story of Jesus' baptism.

118 Dallas Willard's paraphrases of Jesus words in Matthew 28:18-20.

119 Steve M. Nash, "Are These the 33 Most Common Fears?" (SelfHelpCollective.com). The list came from the most common Internet searches.

120 E. James Wilder, Anna Kang, John and Sungshim Loppnow, *Joyful Journey: Listening to Immanuel* (Life Model Works: 2015), chapter 5.

121 Eugene Peterson, *Christ Plays in Ten Thousand Places: A Conversation in Spiritual Theology* (William B. Eerdmans Publishing Co: 2005). "Perichoresis" is the Greek word for "dance around" that the ancients writers use to describe the Trinity.

122 Rick Richardson, *Experiencing Healing Prayer: How God Turns Our Hurts Into Wholeness* (IVP: 2005).

123 *Ibid*, pp. 95-96.